Learning AndEngine

Design and create Android games with the simple but powerful tool AndEngine

Martin Varga

BIRMINGHAM - MUMBAI

Learning AndEngine

First published: September 2014

Production reference: 2121114

Published by Packt Publishing Ltd.
Livery Place
35 Livery Street
Birmingham B3 2PB, UK.

ISBN 978-1-78398-596-8

www.packtpub.com

Cover image by Martin Varga (android@kul.is)

Credits

Author
Martin Varga

Reviewers
Jafar Abdulrasoul [Jimmar]
Rafay Ali
Sergio Viudes Carbonell
Bret Hudson

Commissioning Editor
Kartikey Pandey

Acquisition Editor
James Jones

Content Development Editor
Sharvari Tawde

Technical Editors
Tanvi Bhatt
Taabish Khan
Faisal Siddiqui

Copy Editors
Janbal Dharmaraj
Sayanee Mukherjee
Deepa Nambiar
Laxmi Subramanian

Project Coordinator
Judie Jose

Proofreaders
Simran Bhogal
Paul Hindle

Indexers
Tejal Soni
Priya Subramani

Graphics
Ronak Dhruv
Abhinash Sahu

Production Coordinator
Komal Ramchandani

Cover Work
Komal Ramchandani

About the Author

Martin Varga is a professional Java developer with a passion for teaching and developing mobile games. He has worked as a senior software engineer in several domains, including telecommunications, mentoring juniors and leading teams of developers. When it was announced that Java will be the language of choice for the Android mobile platform, he seized the opportunity and started his indie game developer career.

He is the author of *Mr. Dandelion's Adventures*, an Android game made with AndEngine, and a few other games used in his tutorials, which are published on his website `http://android.kul.is`. Alongside the tutorials, he is also trying to promote other indie developers' games and writing game reviews. He's an active member of the AndEngine community and several game development websites, answering questions of newcomers in the indie game development scene daily.

Acknowledgments

First, I'd like to thank Packt Publishing for giving me an opportunity to create something as wonderful as a new book. I must mention Anish Sukumaran, who found me, and then James Jones, Aaron Lazar, and Sharvari Tawde, who helped me on my path from a person who had no idea how to write a book to a person who actually wrote one.

I would also like to thank all members of the game development community who helped me in my humble beginnings. Thanks to Nicolas, for creating AndEngine and making it easy to start; Matthew from `http://www.matim-dev.com/`, for his tutorials that I used to create my first game in AndEngine; and Flavien and Michał, for their contributions to AndEngine, their tutorials, and their games that motivated me.

Finally, I would like to thank all my friends and family who supported me during the writing of this book and during the period when I broke a bone in my foot and had to stay at home for nearly three months. There are too many of them to list, but you know who you are. Special thanks to Melissa who gave me the most valuable feedback during the making of my first game, helped me to actually finish it, and later drove me around when I was not mobile myself.

About the Reviewers

Jafar Abdulrasoul [Jimmar] is a computer engineer, Android developer, and game developer from Kuwait, who has worked on a couple of games on different platforms using various technologies such as AndEngine, cocos2d, and Unity 3D.

Jafar began his programming journey while in high school, and later ventured out to seek more knowledge in this field by getting an engineering degree, while working on personal projects, including Android applications and game development, on the side. He was also one of the reviewers for *AndEngine for Android Game Development Cookbook*, *Jayme Schroeder and Brian Broyles*, *Packt Publishing*.

To Hime, for showing up in my life and giving it a new purpose.

Rafay Ali is a Computer Science graduate from the University of Karachi, currently working as a senior software engineer at KoderLabs. Besides having two years of experience as a Java developer, he has worked on a couple of languages and tools, including C++, C#, JavaScript, Ruby, Android, and Unity 3D. He loves programming computer games and prototypes new game ideas as a hobby. When he's not working, he can be found on Steam, placing wards in *Dota 2*.

Sergio Viudes Carbonell is a 31-year-old software developer from Elche, Spain. He develops apps and video games for the Web, iOS, and Android.

He has been playing video games since his childhood. He started playing with his brother's Spectrum when he was five years old. When he bought his first PC (well, his parents did), he was 14 years old and started learning computer programming, computer drawing, and music composing (using the famous *FastTracker 2*). When he finished high school, he studied Computer Science at the University of Alicante.

His interest in mobile devices started with his first smartphone 12 years ago (2002), when he bought the first Symbian device from Nokia, the Nokia 7650. He really liked the idea that he could develop software that can run everywhere. So, along with his studies and his job, he started creating simple mobile apps for his phone. He really enjoys developing apps for mobile devices, composing music, drawing, and of course, playing video games. So, he decided to put all his hobbies together and develop his first video game for his favorite mobile platform, Android.

So far, Sergio has released three games, several apps, and he continues developing apps and games not only for Android, but also for iOS and the Web.

Sergio was one of the reviewers for *AndEngine for Android Game Development Cookbook*, *Jayme Schroeder and Brian Broyles*, *Packt Publishing* and *Mobile Game Design Essentials*, *Dr. Claudio Scolastici and David Nolte*, *Packt Publishing*.

I would like to thank Nicolas Gramlich for creating AndEngine and Martin Varga for writing this book. Special thanks go to my wife, Fani, who encourages and supports me every day.

Bret Hudson began his programming adventure at the age of 12, starting out with a small program called *Game Maker*, and quickly expanding to developing web applications, software, and mobile apps. He has experience in over 15 programming and scripting languages as well as knowledge of a multitude of types of database software.

www.PacktPub.com

Support files, eBooks, discount offers, and more

You might want to visit www.PacktPub.com for support files and downloads related to your book.

Did you know that Packt offers eBook versions of every book published, with PDF and ePub files available? You can upgrade to the eBook version at www.PacktPub.com and as a print book customer, you are entitled to a discount on the eBook copy. Get in touch with us at service@packtpub.com for more details.

At www.PacktPub.com, you can also read a collection of free technical articles, sign up for a range of free newsletters and receive exclusive discounts and offers on Packt books and eBooks.

http://PacktLib.PacktPub.com

Do you need instant solutions to your IT questions? PacktLib is Packt's online digital book library. Here, you can access, read and search across Packt's entire library of books.

Why subscribe?

- Fully searchable across every book published by Packt
- Copy and paste, print and bookmark content
- On demand and accessible via web browser

Free access for Packt account holders

If you have an account with Packt at www.PacktPub.com, you can use this to access PacktLib today and view nine entirely free books. Simply use your login credentials for immediate access.

Table of Contents

Preface

Android has become the number one platform for mobile phones and tablets, and its popularity is still rising. Mobile game markets have become a great place for both professionals and indie game developers to present their games.

AndEngine was created by Nicolas Gramlich to ease the development of 2D games for Android devices. Since the beginning, AndEngine helped to create many successful games such as *Traktor Digger*, *Construction City*, and *Bad Roads*.

AndEngine is a full-featured open source engine. Its advantage is its simplicity. It is complete and makes creating any 2D game possible, and yet it is still easy to use. Moreover, AndEngine lets programmers use any part of the underlying Android SDK with no limitations.

Learning AndEngine is meant to teach the basics of AndEngine. It's a step-by-step guide to creating a simple game. Through the tutorial, all the basic features of AndEngine are presented in a concise way, making it easy to follow. The book starts with the installation of the required software, making a blueprint of the game, and follows with gradually adding features to the game as the readers learn them. Finally, a game is polished and released for a beta test in the most popular Android application store, the Google Play store.

The AndEngine source code exists in three versions. This book deals with the latest and most commonly used branch called the GLES2 — AnchorCenter branch. It uses a newer graphics library, and it is stable and complete.

What this book covers

Chapter 1, *Setting Up an AndEngine Project*, introduces AndEngine and guides you through the installation of all the necessary software. At the end of the chapter, an empty AndEngine skeleton application is created.

Chapter 2, Game Concept and Assets, introduces the idea of the game that will be created. It begins with outlining the game rules, followed by gathering the game assets and scene diagram, and ends with a completed blueprint for the game.

Chapter 3, From Assets to Entities, explains loading the assets into memory and how to use them in a game. It shows a basic way to display an image on the screen by creating a game entity. It also explains the basic terms and different ways of storing images in memory, considering memory and quality requirements.

Chapter 4, HUD and Text Display, deals with loading fonts, national alphabets, and outputting text. It also explains heads-up display (HUD) and its usage in a game. The way to store characters and most common problems associated with it are explained as well.

Chapter 5, Basic Interactions, teaches you about basic animation and controls in AndEngine. Accelerometer and touchscreen are introduced along with collision detection. In this chapter, the game becomes interactive.

Chapter 6, Physics, introduces the AndEngine Box2D extension that takes care of physics simulation. Accelerometer readings are combined with procedural animation governed by the physics engine to create a better way of controlling the main character.

Chapter 7, Detecting Collisions and Reacting to Events, adds more interactivity and uses the physics engine's optimized collision detection. Game events are created and handled and playing sounds is explained too.

Chapter 8, Advanced Physics, introduces concepts that are not necessary for the game, but nevertheless important. Multiple fixture bodies that can make simulation more precise and realistic are introduced. Collision filtering and its use as an optimization technique is described. Finally, all physics engine joints are listed and explained.

Chapter 9, Adding a Menu and Splash Scene, describes exactly what the title suggests. In this chapter, a splash scene that is shown at the start of the game is added and a way to load resources in the background is described. Also, a simple menu scene is added as an entry point to the game.

Chapter 10, Polishing the Game, explores a few ways to polish the game and make it more interesting by adding music, more animations, and some special effects. A standalone fire and smoke particle engine example is created.

Chapter 11, Testing, Publishing, and What's Next, shares insights about joining a community of developers, user testing, debugging, and publishing the game.

What you need for this book

Learning AndEngine is meant for complete beginners in Android game development, but you should know the fundamentals of Java programming. Having some knowledge of the Android platform is beneficial but not required and no knowledge of AndEngine is expected.

All the required software applications are open source and can be obtained for free from the Internet. Therefore, an Internet connection is required. The first chapter of the book helps you download the software and set your environment.

To follow the tutorial in this book, you should own an Android phone or tablet and a PC or a Mac that is able to run the Eclipse IDE and Android SDK. The examples can be run on an Android emulator but it is not recommended.

Who this book is for

If you are an aspiring game developer who is looking for a quick way into the Android game developer world, this is the book for you! This book is most beneficial for those who haven't created any games yet. More advanced users who have made a game in AndEngine already will most likely find the book to be very basic.

Conventions

In this book, you will find a number of styles of text that distinguish between different kinds of information. Here are some examples of these styles, and an explanation of their meaning.

Code words in text, database table names, folder names, filenames, file extensions, pathnames, dummy URLs, user input, and Twitter handles are shown as follows: "The versionName value will be displayed in the store listing."

A block of code is set as follows:

```
@Override
public void populate() {
  ...
  engine.enableAccelerationSensor(activity, this);
}
```

When we wish to draw your attention to a particular part of a code block, the relevant lines or items are set in bold:

```
if (player.isDead()) {
  endGameText.setVisible(true);
  if (score > activity.getHiScore()) {
    activity.setHiScore(score);
  }
}
```

Any command-line input or output is written as follows:

```
adb install LearningAndEngine.apk
```

New terms and **important words** are shown in bold. Words that you see on the screen, in menus or dialog boxes for example, appear in the text like this: "The option is located in the main button bar and in the **Window** menu."

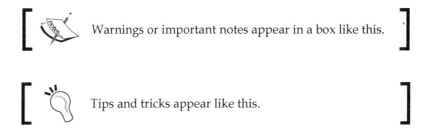

Warnings or important notes appear in a box like this.

Tips and tricks appear like this.

Reader feedback

Feedback from our readers is always welcome. Let us know what you think about this book—what you liked or may have disliked. Reader feedback is important for us to develop titles that you really get the most out of.

To send us general feedback, simply send an e-mail to feedback@packtpub.com, and mention the book title via the subject of your message.

If there is a topic that you have expertise in and you are interested in either writing or contributing to a book, see our author guide on www.packtpub.com/authors.

Customer support

Now that you are the proud owner of a Packt book, we have a number of things to help you to get the most from your purchase.

Downloading the example code

You can download the example code files for all Packt books you have purchased from your account at `http://www.packtpub.com`. If you purchased this book elsewhere, you can visit `http://www.packtpub.com/support` and register to have the files e-mailed directly to you.

Downloading the color images of this book

We also provide you a PDF file that has color images of the screenshots/diagrams used in this book. The color images will help you better understand the changes in the output. You can download this file from: `https://www.packtpub.com/sites/default/files/downloads/5968OS_ColoredImages.pdf`.

Errata

Although we have taken every care to ensure the accuracy of our content, mistakes do happen. If you find a mistake in one of our books—maybe a mistake in the text or the code—we would be grateful if you would report this to us. By doing so, you can save other readers from frustration and help us improve subsequent versions of this book. If you find any errata, please report them by visiting `http://www.packtpub.com/submit-errata`, selecting your book, clicking on the **errata submission form** link, and entering the details of your errata. Once your errata are verified, your submission will be accepted and the errata will be uploaded on our website, or added to any list of existing errata, under the Errata section of that title. Any existing errata can be viewed by selecting your title from `http://www.packtpub.com/support`.

Piracy

Piracy of copyright material on the Internet is an ongoing problem across all media. At Packt, we take the protection of our copyright and licenses very seriously. If you come across any illegal copies of our works, in any form, on the Internet, please provide us with the location address or website name immediately so that we can pursue a remedy.

Please contact us at copyright@packtpub.com with a link to the suspected pirated material.

We appreciate your help in protecting our authors, and our ability to bring you valuable content.

Questions

You can contact us at questions@packtpub.com if you are having a problem with any aspect of the book, and we will do our best to address it.

1
Setting Up an AndEngine Project

In this chapter, we are going to develop an empty AndEngine application that will serve as a base for a game. First, we will discuss prerequisites and download and install the required software. You will also learn where to get the latest and stable AndEngine libraries from. Lastly, we are going to create and implement a simple Android application that uses AndEngine libraries and then run it.

It doesn't matter on which platform you develop the project as long as you can install the Java **Software Development Kit (SDK)** and **Android SDK** there. However, AndEngine is not a multiplatform framework because applications created with AndEngine can run only on an **Android device** or inside an **Android emulator**.

Prerequisites

Android applications are simply Java applications running inside an Android virtual machine called **Dalvik**. You will encounter this name when compiling and running the application. The final compiled code is not fully compatible with the Oracle Java Virtual Machine, but for the purpose of this book, you are only expected to know basic Java programming.

You will need the following software and hardware:

- Windows XP, Vista, 7, or 8; Linux (Ubuntu is recommended); or Mac OS 10.5.8 or a later operating system
- Java SDK
- Android SDK with the ADT bundle
- An Android device

You should already know how to install the Java SDK (JDK) and keep it up to date. The Android SDK requires at least JDK 6. You can use higher versions if available. Always use the latest update for security and compatibility reasons.

It is important to use JDK and not just the **Java Runtime Environment (JRE)** for development. It is also a requirement of Android SDK. Make sure the JAVA_HOME environment variable is set to the correct folder.

Android SDK contains the Eclipse **Integrated Development Environment (IDE)** with preinstalled plugins and Android platform tools. Using the latest version of Android SDK is recommended.

If you have used Eclipse before, you can use your own existing Eclipse installation as well, but then you are required to install the plugins manually on your own.

We are going to download and install Android SDK with the **Android Development Tools (ADT)** bundle in the next section. ADT allows you to install the application to your device and also connect to it in order to get important information such as the **LogCat** console output (text output from installed applications that is not visible to users) and other interesting statistics about running apps.

Your device should be running at least Android 2.2, but using a more recent version is recommended. If you don't own an Android device, you can use an Android emulator for development. However, consider getting a physical device because the behavior of the emulator is different from that of a real phone or tablet. The game might run slower or have problems. Emulators are known to have issues especially with hardware-accelerated graphics. Nothing can replace testing on a real device, and in fact for serious game development, it's a necessity to test on multiple devices.

Downloading and installing the required software

We are going to download and install Android SDK with the ADT bundle first. JDK 6 or later should already be installed and configured on your development machine.

Downloading the Android SDK

Go to http://developer.android.com/sdk/. If you are on Windows, click on the **Download Eclipse ADT with the Android SDK for Windows** button. If you are using a different operating system, the page should autodetect it and offer you the link for your OS. In case it doesn't detect it correctly, there is a link called **VIEW ALL DOWNLOADS AND SIZES** that will expand a list of available platforms. Choose the right platform for you. Be careful when choosing 32-bit or 64-bit software. If you are running a 32-bit Java on a 64-bit system, choose the 32-bit software. Accept the license agreement and save the file to your hard drive. The examples in this chapter are from the 32-bit version for Windows.

 There is another IDE available, Android Studio. However, it is in the early access stage. It is not recommended to use this IDE.

Installing the Android SDK

The downloaded file will be a ZIP archive called something like adt-bundle-windows-x86-20131030.zip. The filename indicates the selected platform and the date of release. To install the software, simply unpack the archive to any folder.

 If you have decided to use an existing Eclipse IDE, expand the **GET THE SDK FOR AN EXISTING IDE** link and click on the **Download the stand-alone Android SDK tools for Windows** button. Or, download the SDK tools for appropriate platforms from the **VIEW ALL DOWNLOADS AND SIZES** link. After that, follow the instructions at http://developer.android.com/sdk/installing/.

You should find the following in the folder where you have unpacked the archive:

* The eclipse folder
* The sdk folder
* The SDK Manager.exe file

First, run the `SDK Manager.exe` file. It might take a while to start, and it doesn't show any splash screen. You will be presented with a window similar to the one in the following screenshot:

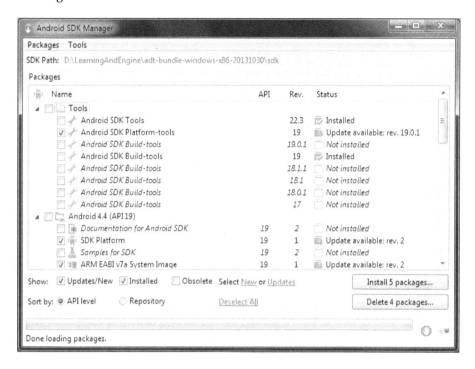

Check for any packages that have updates available. Note that you only need the latest SDK, which at the time this book was written was SDK 19 for Android 4.4. The latest version is always bundled with the Android SDK. You should also check the **Google USB Driver** option.

Every SDK version allows you to write applications that can be deployed to any Android version. If you use a function from an SDK version that is not available in an older Android SDK, the method will not be executed and you will get a warning or an exception. Be careful with that because the code will compile and deploy!

Optionally, you can install the Android emulator system images for older Android versions. This is useful for testing. However, AndEngine can't be deployed to an Android emulator with Android versions 2.x. For now, do not install anything else but the updates and the USB driver. Install the selected packages and close the SDK manager. The installation might take a while, because the packages are downloaded from the Internet.

Configuring the Eclipse IDE

Now, run the Eclipse IDE. From the `eclipse` folder, run the `eclipse.exe` file. After the splash, the first thing you will see is the workspace selection window. This is shown in the following screenshot:

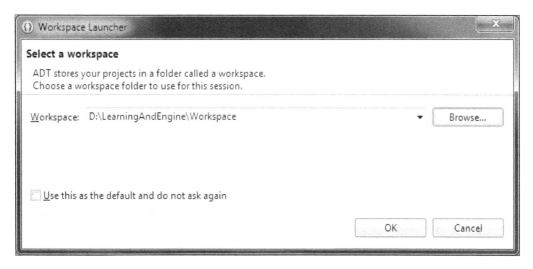

If you have never worked with Eclipse, note that a workspace is both a virtual space on your screen (the layout) and a directory where your projects and some metadata that Eclipse keeps about your projects are stored. Choose any directory you want, but make sure it is one with easy access. You can have multiple workspaces. If you check the **Use this as the default and do not ask again** checkbox, you will be working with this workspace by default and this dialog box won't appear again at the start.

> The workspace selection dialog box is always available by navigating to **File** | **Switch Workspace** menu in Eclipse.

After the start, close the **Welcome** screen and you will be presented with the Eclipse default layout. Parts of the layout can be dragged and dropped to different locations. Also, you can have different perspectives (presets of the opened windows and tabs) for each workspace. We will be using the Java perspective for most of the time but we will also use **Dalvik Debug Monitor Server** (**DDMS**) and the **Debug** perspective for debugging and tuning our application. The perspectives are available by navigating to **Window** | **Open Perspective**.

Stay in the Java perspective, but go to **Window** | **Show View** | **Other…** and search for **LogCat**, as shown in the following screenshot:

LogCat is a log console. The Android system has a logging system that allows developers to print categorized text messages to LogCat from their apps. This is very useful for game developers because the text output to the screen can be very limited. The ADT takes care of getting the LogCat output from the connected Android device.

The Eclipse IDE can be a bit difficult to grasp from the start. However, as a Java developer, you have probably used it before or have used a similar one. Most of the IDEs nowadays are very similar. Try to familiarize yourself with Eclipse before proceeding to the next step.

Getting the AndEngine libraries

AndEngine is an open source game engine and the sources are licensed under Apache License Version 2.0. This not only allows us to use AndEngine in both free and commercial games, but it also gives us a chance to inspect or alter the source code. The old way of adding AndEngine to an Android application was to add compiled **Java ARchive** (**JAR**) files to your app. This is no longer necessary as you can add AndEngine as a library project.

The author of AndEngine, *Nicolas Gramlich*, decided to store the whole engine inside GitHub. Git is a **version control system** (**VCS**) for source codes and GitHub is a hosting website for Git repositories. A VCS allows you to not only store your sources, but also to store every version of each file. This is of course useful when you need to see the history of your changes or collaborate with more people.

A repository is a logical unit. As a rule of thumb, one repository contains one project. A repository has its address and history separated from other repositories. A repository in GitHub can be forked (creates your own copy with your own history), cloned (creates a version on your machine linked with the repository), or zipped and downloaded locally.

 For more general information about AndEngine, visit the official website at www.andengine.org.

Selecting the correct branch

Android uses **OpenGL ES** to display accelerated graphics. OpenGL ES is a free API for full-function 2D and 3D graphics on embedded systems. There are several versions of OpenGL ES, namely versions 1.x, 2.x, and recently 3.x.

A repository can also contain multiple branches. Think of a branch as an alternative version of the project. AndEngine is split into three branches. The GLES1 branch uses OpenGL ES 1.0 and it is the oldest. I don't recommend using it. GLES2 is newer and GLES2-AnchorCenter is the newest. They both use OpenGL ES 2. Use the GLES2-AnchorCenter branch if you haven't used AndEngine before. The GLES2-AnchorCenter branch's biggest difference from the GLES2 branch is the fact that point [0, 0] is now in the lower-left corner of the screen. This is the same as in OpenGL and that's why it's recommended.

For the purpose of this book, we are going to exclusively use the GLES2-AnchorCenter branch.

AndEngine repositories

AndEngine is split into a main project simply called AndEngine and many extensions called, for example, AndEngineMultiplayerExtension, which are dependent on the main project. Each project resides in its own repository.

For our game, we need the main AndEngine project and a 2D physics extension called AndEnginePhysicsBox2DExtension. This extension adds a very popular 2D physics simulation framework called Box2D to AndEngine. A lot of popular games use this framework.

There is also a repository called AndEngineExamples. It is not an extension but an application that includes all of the other AndEngine libraries and extensions and illustrates their use.

If you download all the extensions and the `AndEngineExamples` project, you can build the AndEngineExamples app and run it on your Android device. An older version is also available online on the Google Play store at `https://play.google.com/store/apps/details?id=org.anddev.andengine.examples`.

Downloading the sources

You can download the sources from Nicolas Gramlich's original repository at `https://github.com/nicolasgramlich/`.

However, there is a danger that the codes will be changed any time in the future. For that reason, I recommend to download the sources from my forked repository, which is guaranteed to work with the sources in this book.

The easiest way is to download the complete repository as a ZIP archive, which can be done with the help of the following steps:

1. Browse to `https://github.com/sm4/`, switch to the **Repositories** tab, and select **AndEngine**. Notice the drop-down menu titled **branch**. Make sure **GLES2-AnchorCenter** is selected. Alternatively, you can browse directly to the correct branch by going to `https://github.com/sm4/AndEngine/tree/GLES2-AnchorCenter`.

2. The following screenshot is what you should see now:

3. Click on the **Download ZIP** button. A file named
   `AndEngine-GLES2-AnchorCenter.zip` will be downloaded.

4. Unpack it in the workspace directory you selected when
   configuring the Eclipse IDE. Note that the directory is called
   `AndEngine-GLES2-AnchorCenter`. It contains the name of the
   project and the branch name as well. Rename the directory to `AndEngine`.

5. Repeat the process for the `AndEnginePhysicsBox2DExtension`
   repository. It can be downloaded from `https://github.com/sm4/`
   `AndEnginePhysicsBox2DExtension/tree/GLES2-AnchorCenter`.

6. Don't forget to rename the directory to `AndEnginePhysicsBox2DExtension`
   only. You should have two folders in your workspace directory: `AndEngine`
   and `AndEnginePhysicsBox2DExtension`.

 If you decide to use a different branch, remember that extensions
used must be from the same branch as the main project.

Adding AndEngine to the Eclipse IDE

In Eclipse, navigate to **File | Import** and choose **Existing Projects into Workspace**
(under the **General** folder). Browse to your workspace directory. You should see two
projects. Check them both and import them by clicking on the **Finish** button. This is
shown in the following screenshot:

If you have installed the ADT bundle with Android SDK 19, you should see no errors. In case there are errors, try cleaning and building all projects again. Simply click on the **Project** drop-down menu in Eclipse's main menu and select the **Clean…** option while having the **Build Automatically** option checked.

It is possible that when you were installing the ADT bundle, it contained a different SDK version from 19, or maybe you are, for some other reason, using a different version. In that case, you will see messages like the following in the console:

```
[2014-01-14 15:36:11 - AndEngine] Unable to resolve target
   'android-19'
```

Right-click on the project, select the **Properties** option, and then choose the **Android** option. Make sure that the Android SDK version of your choice (or simply the latest) is selected. This is shown in the following screenshot. You will probably have to clean the project to make the error disappear. We have to do this because the project was saved with SDK 19 selected. Do it for both projects.

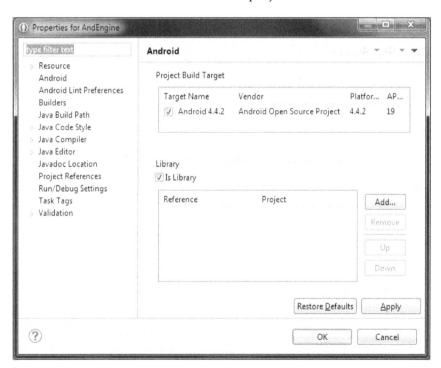

Creating a new application

We will first create an empty Android application project and later add the AndEngine libraries.

Creating a simple Android application

To create a simple Android application, we will follow these steps:

1. Go to **File | New | Android Application Project in Eclipse**. You will be presented with the window shown in the following screenshot:

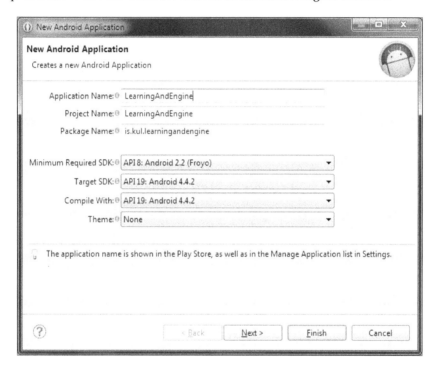

- ° **Application Name**: This is visible under the app's icon on your phone. When creating a real application/game, give it a meaningful name. Let's say your game is called *Awesome Football Manager*. You can simply put this in the **Application Name** field, but on the phone, you will probably see only *Awesome Foo...* under the icon, due to the limit of characters that can be displayed.

○ **Project Name**: This is just the project name in Eclipse, and it is how your APK (Android Application Package—the final archive to be deployed to the device) will be named. I recommend using a single word derived from your application name.

○ **Package Name**: This is used for your Java code and it is also a unique identifier for the Google Play store. Make sure your chosen package name is not taken! If you have your own domain, put it there (backwards). If you don't have one, imagine that you do and what it would look like. My domain is `kul.is`; therefore, my package starts with `is.kul` and the full package name will be `is.kul.learningandengine`.

○ **Minimum Required SDK**: This is simply the lowest Android version that you are going to support. AndEngine works well with SDK 8, but if you are going to use big textures, you might run into problems. It is always a trade-off between supporting as many devices as possible and making sure that the application will work on all supported devices. The lower the SDK, the more problems you can expect and the more devices you should test. On the other hand, more devices will be supported and you will reach a broader user base. Android 2.2 and 2.3 are still used today.

○ **Target SDK** and **Compile With**: For these, pick the highest available SDK (19). You should own a device with the target SDK, or test the application in the emulator.

○ **Theme**: For this, select **None**. Your activity theme won't be visible, so don't bother with it. Our game in AndEngine will use an overlay view that will cover the whole available screen.

2. Click on the **Next** button to continue the application creation wizard.

3. On the next page, uncheck the **Create custom launcher icon** option. This option will launch another wizard where you can upload an image that would serve as your app icon in the store and on the device. We will keep the default green Android icon for now.

4. Keep the **Create activity** option checked. An activity is a single, focused thing that the user can do (in our case, *play the game*, but it can be for example, *check emails* or *record voice*), and it represents the presentation layer of an Android application. It is also a Java class that extends the `Activity` class from the Android library. Have a look at the following screenshot:

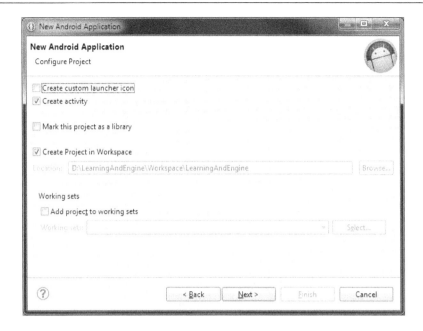

5. Click on the **Next** button to advance to the **Create activity** page as shown in the following screenshot. Leave everything as it is and click on the **Next** button again. We are creating a blank activity, but in fact, it doesn't matter. We are going to change the activity anyway. We are using this option in order to get the `Activity` class created for us in the right package.

6. The last page allows us to name the activity and the layout. We are not going to work with the layout in this book, so you can leave it as it is. We are going to name the activity `GameActivity`. This is shown in the following screenshot:

7. Click on the **Finish** button to close the wizard. A new project will appear in the Eclipse **Project Explorer** window (the tab on the left). You can run the project now, but your device must be configured properly. First, plug in your Android device.

Device configuration

You need to enable the **USB debugging** option under **Developer options** on your phone or tablet in order to deploy the application from Eclipse. The configuration differs across Android versions, and it can even differ for the same version on a different device or brand.

Before Honeycomb

Honeycomb is the codename for Android 3.0. In versions prior to Honeycomb, the developer options are located under **Settings** | **Applications** | **Development**.

Honeycomb until Ice Cream Sandwich

You will find the **Developer options** button under **Settings** | **Developer options** in the **System** subsection.

Jelly Bean and later

The developer options are hidden starting with Android 4.2. You need to use the following trick to activate the option:

1. Go to **Settings** | **About phone**.
2. Scroll down to the **Build number** option.
3. Tap on this option seven times. On the third tap, you should see the message about four taps remaining to become a developer.
4. Go back to the **Settings** window.
5. You should see the **Developer options** menu item in your **Settings** window.

Check the **USB debugging** option. This should be all that is required to upload the application from Eclipse to your device.

 Consider turning on the **Unknown sources** option under the **Security** option as well. Basically, it means you can install APKs from other sources than the Google Play store. This is useful for testing when you upload a production APK directly from your development machine to the device. The development versions of apps are allowed thanks to the **USB debugging** option.

Running the application

Connect the device using a USB cable. You should see a notification of **USB debugging connected** on your phone or tablet.

Finally, in Eclipse, select the project and click on the drop-down arrow next to the run icon in the Eclipse top bar. Navigate to **Run As | Android Application**. This is shown in the following screenshot:

A pop-up window named **Android Device Chooser** will show the list of connected devices. Select your device. You can also check the **Use same device for future launches** option, which will remember your device for this session and will use it as the default target when you run the application the next time. Your device must run the project's minimum Android SDK or higher.

 If you don't have a physical Android device, the **Android Device Chooser** window will allow you to define a virtual device using the Android emulator.

Have a look at the following screenshot:

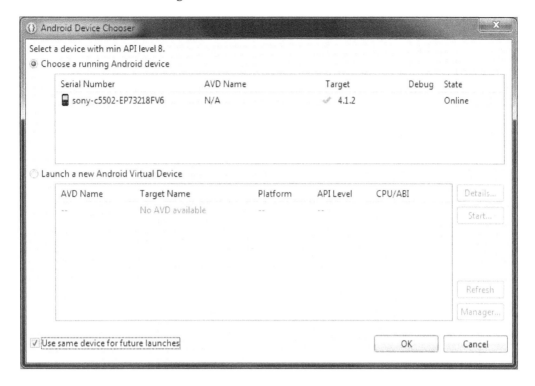

After clicking on the **OK** button, Eclipse will build the application and create an APK. All applications have to be signed using a certificate before publishing to the Google Play store. For development purposes, all APKs are signed using a debug certificate.

The APK is then uploaded to the device and the main activity, in our case GameActivity, is started. You should see a simple one-screen application with **Hello World** text on the display. This is a default Hello World Android application created by Eclipse.

Adding AndEngine

We need to add the AndEngine and AndEnginePhysicsBox2DExtension libraries to our app and change the GameActivity.

Adding the required projects

AndEngine and all the extensions are library projects. That means they can be added to our application as dependencies, similar to adding an external library JAR file. Eclipse will then build and package the library project along with our application to the final APK.

Right-click on the project, select **Properties**, and choose **Android**. Click on the **Add** button in the **Library** subsection and select **AndEngine**. Also add the **AndEnginePhysicsBox2DExtension** project similarly. This is shown in the following screenshot:

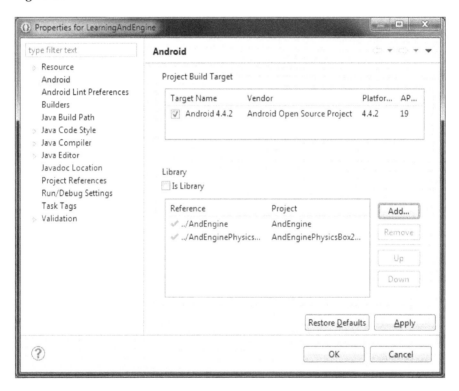

Changing the GameActivity to an AndEngine activity

AndEngine extends the basic Android `Activity` class because it needs to take care of a lot of initializing and loading of resources for the game engine. AndEngine gives us several hooks that we can use to perform our own initializations.

Understanding the activity lifecycle

It is important to understand the lifecycle of an Android application and activities. For a basic game, a single activity is usually enough, making things simpler. The following diagram describes the most basic activity lifecycle:

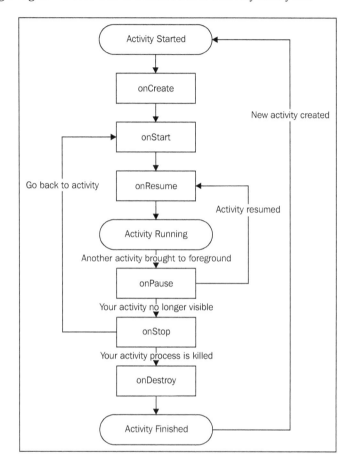

When you start your application, it goes through different states and the callback methods onCreate, onStart, and onResume are called. Notice that the onResume method is called even on the first start.

An activity is paused typically when the screen is locked or a dialog activity is brought to the front. Imagine a low battery warning for example. An activity is stopped when another activity completely covers your activity. This can be an incoming call. Note that the onStop method doesn't have to be called. This can happen when the system doesn't have enough resources for another activity and decides to kill your activity right away. The final method, onDestroy, is called when your activity is finished and cleared from the memory. Again, it is not guaranteed to be called.

The lifecycle is more complex than this and there are even more hooks that can be overridden and used. For our purposes, this will be enough. In fact, AndEngine takes care of most of the methods and gives us a few convenient methods to use instead.

The BaseGameActivity class

Our GameActivity class extends the BaseGameActivity class, which implements basic game activity behavior for us. For example, it implements the onCreate method that configures the engine and the surface view. The surface view is a dedicated drawing surface for our game that we can use through AndEngine.

When you created the empty GameActivity, it looked like the following code (it can differ based on the Eclipse and ADT versions):

```
package is.kul.learningandengine;

import android.os.Bundle;
import android.app.Activity;
import android.view.Menu;

public class GameActivity extends Activity {

  @Override
  protected void onCreate(Bundle savedInstanceState) {
    super.onCreate(savedInstanceState);
    setContentView(R.layout.activity_game);
  }

  @Override
  public boolean onCreateOptionsMenu(Menu menu) {
    // Inflate the menu; this adds items to the action bar if it
      is present.
    getMenuInflater().inflate(R.menu.game, menu);
    return true;
  }

}
```

Delete both the onCreate and onCreateOptionsMenu methods. Change the parent of the GameActivity class from android.app.Activity to org.andengine. ui.activity.BaseGameActivity.

BaseGameActivity is an abstract class, and it will make you implement the onCreateEngineOptions, onCreateResources, onCreateScene, and onPopulateScene methods. The lifecycle methods are all handled by AndEngine.

The onCreateEngineOptions method

1. First, define the onCreateEngineOptions method. This method is called from the onCreate method and it is run first. You are supposed to configure AndEngine's engine in this method. The following is a typical example:

```
public static final int CAMERA_WIDTH = 480;
public static final int CAMERA_HEIGHT = 800;


@Override
public EngineOptions onCreateEngineOptions() {
  Camera camera = new Camera(0, 0, CAMERA_WIDTH,
    CAMERA_HEIGHT);
  IResolutionPolicy resolutionPolicy = new
    FillResolutionPolicy();
  EngineOptions engineOptions = new EngineOptions(true,
    ScreenOrientation.PORTRAIT_FIXED, resolutionPolicy,
    camera);
  engineOptions.getAudioOptions().setNeedsMusic(true).
    setNeedsSound(true);
  engineOptions.setWakeLockOptions(WakeLockOptions.
    SCREEN_ON);
  Debug.i("Engine configured");
  return engineOptions;
}
```

We have defined two static constants that define the resolution of our view port. AndEngine will then take care of scaling the final picture on the device.

2. In the method itself, we start with the camera definition. The Camera object defines the part of the scene that will be visible. It takes four parameters: the first two are the bottom-left coordinates in the scene and the third and fourth are the width and height of the visible area.

3. Next, we define a resolution policy. The Android platform suffers from a variety of different screen sizes and ratios. AndEngine tries to deal with this by letting you specify one resolution and then scaling the resulting picture to any device.

4. You don't need to care whether the screen size of the phone is bigger or smaller than your desired resolution. AndEngine can enlarge your scene or shrink the picture. You place your objects at coordinates in your resolution. However, you still have to hint AndEngine about how the resulting picture should be scaled, and that's what the resolution policy is for.

5. In the example, we are using the `FillResolutionPolicy`. As the name suggests, this policy fills the whole screen with your scene. Your picture will be resized but the aspect ratio will not be kept, unless the phone and your scene have the same ratio. Pixels can become taller or wider.

6. Then, we create the `EngineOptions` object. This is the final object that will be passed to the engine. It takes four parameters, as follows:

   ° **Fullscreen**: This option is set to `true`, as we want our game to cover the whole screen.

   ° **Screen orientation**: For this, the possible values are `PORTRAIT_SENSOR`, `PORTRAIT_FIXED`, `LANDSCAPE_SENSOR`, and `LANDSCAPE_FIXED`. The sensor variant will flip the picture upside down when you flip the device.

   ° **Resolution policy**: This is explained earlier.

   ° **Camera**: This is explained earlier.

7. We also set the audio options simply to indicate that we will be using both sound and music.

8. Last, we set the wake lock to `SCREEN_ON`. This simply means that the device will not enter sleep mode due to inactivity. This is important because you can have a period in your game without user input when you don't want the screen to turn off by itself. This can be a cutscene for example.

9. The line `Debug.i("Engine configured");` is optional. This will print the **Engine configured** message to LogCat. Use this kind of debug message to check whether the method ran successfully.

> The messages can have different levels: error, warning, info, debug, and verbose. Each level has its own method, such as `Debug.e` or `Debug.d`. These are used to differentiate the severity of the method as LogCat allows filtering by the level. You can use `Debug.i("MyTag", "Engine configured");` in your code to further categorize your messages based on tags.

10. At the end, we return the `engineOptions` object.

The onCreateResources method

The `onCreateResources` method is called after the engine options are created, and it is used to initialize game resources such as graphics, sounds, and music. For now, we leave this method empty.

```
@Override
public void onCreateResources(
  OnCreateResourcesCallback pOnCreateResourcesCallback)
  throws IOException {
  pOnCreateResourcesCallback.onCreateResourcesFinished();
}
```

Notice the `pOnCreateResourcesCallback` parameter. This is used to indicate that you are done loading the resources and the control is given back to the engine. You have to call the `onCreateResourcesFinished` method, otherwise the engine will not continue.

The onCreateScene method

The `onCreateScene` method is called from the `onCreateResourcesCallback` object when you call the `Finished` method. It is used to create a **scene** object or objects.

Every displayable object in AndEngine is an entity. That includes the scene, which is the parent of all the other entities currently displayed. The engine can display one scene at a time, and you will typically want to define multiple scenes, such as a menu scene and a game scene. You can also have child scenes, which are used to display a pause screen or a game over screen.

The following code describes the simplest scene. We only create an empty scene object and set its background to cyan color.

```
@Override
public void onCreateScene(OnCreateSceneCallback
  pOnCreateSceneCallback)
  throws IOException {
  Scene scene = new Scene();
  scene.getBackground().setColor(Color.CYAN);
  pOnCreateSceneCallback.onCreateSceneFinished(scene);
}
```

Again, you have to call the `Finished` method on the provided callback object to tell the engine you are done creating your scene.

The onPopulateScene method

The `onPopulateScene` method is the final method we need to implement, which is used to populate the scene with entities. For the simplest example, we are not going to add any. Leave the method body empty, but remember to return the `Scene` object. This method is called from the `Scene` callback and you have to call the next callback too. This is described in the following code:

```
@Override
public void onPopulateScene(Scene pScene,
  OnPopulateSceneCallback pOnPopulateSceneCallback)
  throws IOException {
  pOnPopulateSceneCallback.onPopulateSceneFinished();
}
```

> There is an alternative to `BaseGameActivity` called `SimpleBaseGameActivity` which calls the callbacks for you at the end of each of the `onCreateResources`, `onCreateScene`, and `onPopulateScene` methods. It's up to you which one you want to use, but you should understand what the callbacks are doing.

Running the application

Run the application and you should see an empty screen with a cyan background. You can refer to the full source code for this chapter in the code bundle.

Understanding resolution policies

In the previous section, we configured the engine with `FillResolutionPolicy`. Dealing with different screen resolutions can be a big issue, and it is one of the most difficult topics to grasp for beginners. Especially for the first game, you should choose a single resolution and prepare all your graphics assets as if you were showing them in this resolution only. Let the engine deal with scaling and shrinking.

As you have learned before, AndEngine deals with different screen resolutions and rations by using resolution policies. There are several of them, and they are suitable for different scenarios.

Let's say you want to work with a resolution of 800 x 480 px. Your square is 80 x 80 px large. Let's add three of them to the scene. So, this is how you want your scene to look. The bottom-left square is placed at [50, 50]. AndEngine calculates where to display it in different resolutions.

It should look like the following screenshot:

Let's see what this would look like on a Google Nexus 4 using different resolution policies. The Google Nexus 4 has a resolution of 1280 x 768 px.

FixedResolutionPolicy

This policy simply creates a renderable area of specified size. If your screen is 1280 x 768 px like on the Nexus shown in the following screenshot, the 800 x 480 px scene will be centered with a big border. If your screen size is exactly 800 x 480 px, your scene will perfectly fit on your display. If your device has a smaller resolution, the whole scene will be cropped. This policy keeps the aspect ratio of pixels (squares will be squares).

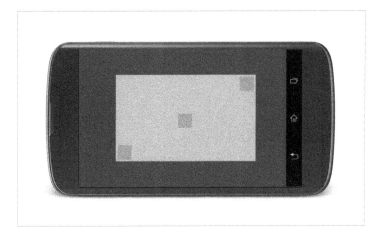

You can of course pass anything to your FixedResolutionPolicy. It doesn't have to be the same as the camera dimensions. You can measure the display size of the device and then manually position all elements based on this measurement. That's what this policy is for.

FillResolutionPolicy

As mentioned earlier, the FillResolutionPolicy fills the screen but can distort the image because it doesn't keep the scene ratio.

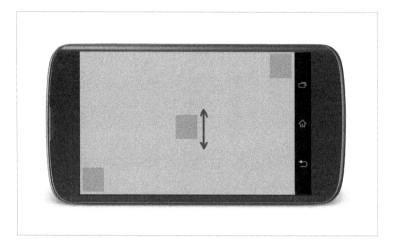

You can see in the previous screenshot that on the Nexus 4, the difference is almost unnoticeable, because 800 x 480 px ratio is about 1.66, and the Nexus 4 screen ratio of 1280 x 768 is 1.66 too. But thanks to the soft buttons in the system bar, the usable portion has roughly 1.56 screen ratio, and that's why the squares are slightly taller.

RelativeResolutionPolicy

You have to pass two floats to this policy, which are the percentages of width and height of the screen you want to use. So, if you pass (1, 1), it means *give me the whole screen* (the same as FillResolutionPolicy).

RatioResolutionPolicy

A ratio policy is probably the most commonly used in the examples. It keeps the aspect ratio and scales your scene to fit one dimension. The other dimension will be padded with the background color of your theme. It will create two bars.

They are highlighted with yellow in the following screenshot:

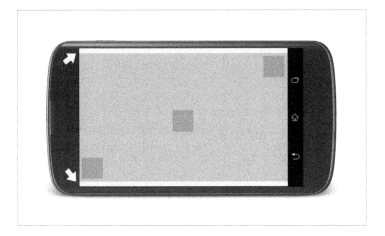

If you set your background theme to be black, the bars will be black. If you use this policy, try to match the theme background color to your game's background.

CropResolutionPolicy

This policy was originally created by user `jgibbs` on the AndEngine forums. He called it `CroppedResolutionPolicy`. You will find a slightly modified version of it in my GitHub repository.

The crop policy is similar to the ratio policy, but instead of padding, it scales the scene while keeping the aspect ratio to cover the whole screen and crops the overflow. See the arrows in the following screenshot pointing to the areas that will be cropped:

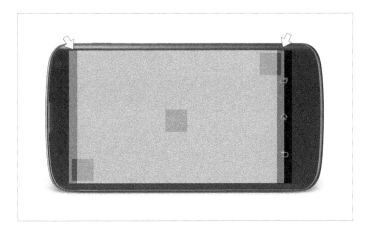

This policy is not the easiest to use. You must place the objects relative to the edges. The center of the screen will still be the center, but you can't simply say: place sprite at [0, 0]. It might be in the overflow on some devices.

Summary

In this chapter, we learned how to set up our environment in order to develop AndEngine games. We saw how to create a new Android application and how to implement a foundation for an AndEngine game. Basic AndEngine parameters were explained. We also covered one of the most difficult and important topics — the resolution policies.

In the next chapter, we will draft our game idea and prepare the graphics, sound, and music assets.

2
Game Concept and Assets

This chapter will introduce the game that we are going to make throughout the course of this book. Even though this is not strictly an AndEngine topic, every game must begin with a concept. We will outline the basic entities and gameplay rules. We will also prepare all the assets needed for the game: graphics, sounds, and music. This chapter will give you an idea of where to get pre-made assets. In the second part of the chapter, we are going to include the assets to our game.

The game concept will be a *Doodle Jump* type of game that illustrates many of the AndEngine features. We are going to create something that is called a game clone. We will use similar rules but our own assets and code. Game clones are often the first witnesses of a new game genre being born.

The game concept

We need to know how our game is going to look before we start coding. It is important to have a basic idea and try to imagine whether this idea will work. For your first game, it's highly recommended to start with something small and possibly something that already exists.

 Do not start with a complex idea. If it is your first game, you will most likely get stuck and have a hard time finishing it. Pick something you can finish in a matter of days.

Start with a pen and paper or some simple graphics software and try to draw the basic screen from the game. The following figure is an example:

The basic idea is very simple. However, let's try to state even the obvious details. This helps us to make sure we don't forget anything. The main goal of the character is to get as high as possible. The score will be calculated from the height reached. The obvious facts are that the game will be played in portrait mode and that there is gravity that pulls our character down. The not so obvious fact is that when the character leaves the screen from the left or right side, we want him to come back on the other side. This is called **wrap around**.

There are randomly generated platforms that he can use as spring boards. The character will be able to pass through the platform upwards, then fall on it, and the platform should propel him up again. This is the key element of the game. See the following illustration:

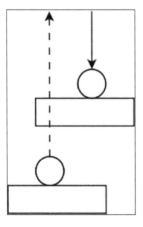

As the character moves upwards, the camera follows him. When the character misses the last platform on the current screen, the game is over. This also means that we have to remove every platform that goes out of view when the view scrolls upwards.

To make the game a little bit more interesting, we can add enemies as well. These will be flies hovering in the air.

Finally, we are going to add some decorations, let's say a couple of clouds.

We are going to include the Box2D physics extension that will take care of gravity and collisions. We can implement these ourselves. This extension is probably overkill for such a simple game. Let's use it anyway to see how physics in games work.

We want to have a sound on each jump and also a sound that will be played when the characters misses the platform and falls down. We also want some background music as well.

Now, let's think about controls. The jump will be triggered automatically as soon as the character touches the platform. How should he move from left to right? There are basically two options. First, we can use touch controls. Either add two buttons to the screen or let the whole left half of the screen be a button to move left and the right half a button to move right. We can also make use of the accelerometer and let the character move by tilting the phone. Both approaches will work. Let's leave this question open for now. AndEngine makes both options very easy to implement.

Identifying the basic entities

Let's review the concept and identify the basic entities in the game. They are as follows:

- Character
- Platform
- Enemy
- Cloud

That's it. For each of the entities, we will need a graphic representation. The character and enemy will be animated. For platforms and clouds, we only want static images.

Getting the assets

Assets are all resources used in a game including graphics, sound, and music. Maps, levels, 3D models, skeleton animations, or any other kind of content in an external file is an asset too.

When making a game, the best approach is, of course, to create a set of original assets made exclusively for your game. However, this might not be possible for different reasons, such as budget. Fortunately, there are plenty of free assets available online for game developers to use.

 Use free assets to create a proof of concept of your game idea before you start investing money in custom-made assets!

You can find a sample list of completely free assets at `http://android.kul.is/p/list-of-free-resources.html`.

 Always check the license of free assets. The license can restrict their commercial use.

We are going to search for all assets in this list. There is one asset pack that is very useful for making a proof of concept game. It is called Open Game Art Bundle, and you will find it at `http://open.commonly.cc/`.

This asset pack is licensed as **Creative Commons Zero** (**CC-0**), which basically means you can use it for any purpose. You can also modify any part of it and redistribute it.

 For more information about Creative Commons licenses, visit `http://creativecommons.org/licenses/`.

Graphics

For our character, enemy, clouds, and platform, we will utilize a set of sprites from Open Game Art Bundle. A sprite is a piece of graphic that can be moved on the screen. The graphic is usually saved in an image file. If there is more than one sprite in the same picture, we call it a sprite sheet. Sprite sheets are very useful, especially when creating animations.

You can see a preview of the sprite sheet, which has been used in several platform games already, in the following screenshot. You might see some parts of it that we are going to use.

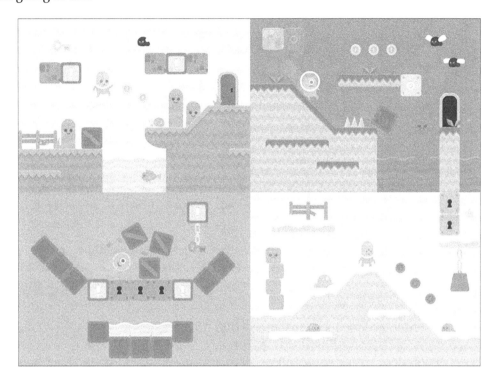

You will find all the following assets in the code bundle.

Graphic formats

AndEngine can load images of any **raster** format that is supported by Android. The raster format means the pixels are stored one by one. When you scale the raster format, you have to compute each new pixel in the scaled version from the existing information. While this is usually not a problem when scaling down the picture, it can produce blurring or unwanted artifacts when scaling up.

The second option is the **vector graphics** format, where lines, curves, rectangles, and so on are stored separately and the image is drawn when needed. The biggest advantage of the vector file format is that it can be scaled indefinitely while keeping the same quality. On the other hand, working with vectors needs more performance; therefore, the vectors are usually **rasterized** before they are used in games. Rasterization is a process in which the vector graphics described as shapes are converted to pixels, usually by rendering them in a selected resolution.

The file size of different formats varies. In the end, all images will be stored in the graphics memory as textures, and it doesn't matter which format is used. However, the file formats influence the storage space needed, quality of the final texture, and load times.

The supported raster formats are the following:

- JPEG
- GIF
- PNG
- BMP
- WebP (Android 4.0 and above)

AndEngine has one extension that allows us to use the SVG vector file format. It rasterizes the SVG file. Vectors are drawn onto a canvas first and then saved into memory as any other raster image.

Each format has its use, advantages, and disadvantages. For an updated list of supported file formats, visit the official Android SDK page at `http://developer.android.com/guide/appendix/media-formats.html`. The formats are described as follows:

- **Joint Photographic Experts Group (JPEG)**: This is the most common **lossy compression** image file format used today. Lossy means it compresses the image by discarding some information. It is important to understand how JPEG works to make full use of it and to know when to avoid it.

  JPEG exploits the imperfections of human vision. First, it reduces the number of colors that are available. Instead of the red, green, and blue components, JPEG stores pixels in YCbCr space, which means one intensity channel and two color components. You can imagine the intensity channel as a black and white representation of the image and the two chroma components as coordinates in a two-dimensional color palette. As the human eye is more sensitive to intensity than to color, the color palette space is shrunk usually by a factor of 2. This is the first loss of information.

  In the next step, the image is cut into 8 x 8 pixel blocks. These are transformed using **Discrete Cosine Transformation** (DCT), which gives us a different representation of the blocks. Instead of 64 pixels, we represent all the blocks as a linear combination of 64 patterns and then reduce the number of possible values of the coefficients of the combination. This is the second loss of information, and it is called quantization. The quality setting of JPEG influences how much the coefficients will be quantized, and therefore how much information will be lost.

Finally, the blocks are losslessly compressed using a compression method similar to the file compression format ZIP.

The JPEG file format doesn't use transparency. It is most useful to represent real-world images and photographs. In a game, you would typically want JPEG to store, for example, a real sky image. JPEG offers the smallest file size for real-world images, but there is always a trade-off with quality. It is not recommended for cartoon graphics.

In the next figure, compare the original cartoon graphic (left) and the result saved as JPEG with very low compression (right). The quantization introduces block artifacts. This example uses extremely strong quantization, but with today's high quality displays, even higher quality compression can be noticeable.

- **Graphics Interchange Format (GIF)**: This used to be a very popular format, and it is going through a renaissance thanks to its animation capability. The format, however, has its limitations. It can only use a 256-color palette with one color reserved for the alpha channel (transparency). It uses lossless compression as well. The file size can be very small but it is not used in games due to the color limitations and also because there is a better file format available. However, it is still supported by Android because it is very popular on the Internet.

- **Bitmap (BMP)**: BMP is losslessly compressed using the **run-length encoding** image file format. This means that same pixels in a row are saved as a color and the length of the series. BMP files tend to be big and they don't have any advantage over PNG.

- **Portable Network Graphics (PNG)**: We will be using the PNG file format for our sprites, and it is also the recommended raster graphics format for cartoon graphics. It uses lossless compression and has an alpha channel (transparency). There are different types of PNG: 8-bit (useful for black and white images) and 24-bit, which can support any number of colors displayable by current screens. The alpha channel in PNG can be missing (saves space), 1-bit (on/off), or 8-bit (256 levels of transparency).

PNG offers a good size to quality ratio. The file size grows with the increasing complexity of the image. PNG doesn't handle photos or cartoon graphics with gradients very well.

- **WebP**: This is a new file format from Google. It offers both lossy and lossless compression and claims to produce smaller file sizes. Its limitation is that it is not as widespread as the other file formats. You might run into compatibility problems on older Android versions. This file format is not recommended to be used with AndEngine.

- **Scalable Vector Graphics** (**SVG**): This is a textual file format. It is very verbose and describes how the image should be drawn. AndEngine has an extension to convert the SVG files to textures. However, it can take quite a lot of time at the start of the game. SVG can be useful for supporting a wide range of devices. However, that is an advanced topic.

The main character

The main character will have the following three animation frames:

- Flying up (jumping)
- Falling on a platform
- Falling below a platform (game over)

In platform games, it is very common to have several frames for animations of walking, running, and so on. Our game is much simpler. We can find all the necessary frames in the existing sprite sheet in the pack. For our purposes, we will cut the needed frames and create our own sheet. Have a look at the following figure:

player.png

The three frames, starting from the left, are:

- Jump
- Fall
- Game over fall

All frames have the same dimensions. While this is not always necessary, it makes things easier. Unless you need memory size optimizations, simply use the same size frames.

Notice that our character is facing only to the right. This is fine because it's very simple to draw the same sprite flipped horizontally, effectively doubling the number of animation frames. This is a common trick in animation.

The background is transparent. Color has been used for illustration purposes only.

The enemy

The enemy will be static, staying in one place. However, we will make it animated; it will flap its wings, which will create an illusion that it is actually hovering. We only need two frames to create such an animation, which are shown in the following figure:

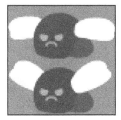

enemy.png

It doesn't matter whether we are creating the sprite sheet horizontally or vertically. You can also have a grid with many frames in one image. Later, we will specify the number of columns and rows for each sprite sheet.

Platform and clouds

We will have two different types of clouds and one platform. The easiest way to save them is to use one file for each sprite. See the following figure:

platform.png

The platform is created from the **tiles** available in Open Game Art Bundle. Two different tiles are used (the left and right halves). We call these images tiles because they are mostly static and make up the floor or walls in a game. You will encounter tiles and tilesets very often in 2D games. Mostly, you will only need a few tiles to create a whole world. Now, have a look at the following figure; it shows our first cloud:

cloud1.png

The following figure shows our second cloud:

cloud2.png

 There are many ways to save the sprites and sprite sheets. There are tools to optimize their placement into a single file. However, for a simple game, don't worry about such optimizations. Make the game first.

Putting it all together

Now, let's try to recreate the initial concept with the graphic assets that we have found. The following screenshot shows how it should look on a phone screen. We are going to create a game that will look pretty much the same.

Notice that we have added a score counter to the top-left corner to complete the design of our game screen.

White color text with black stroke will be visible on any kind of background.

Sounds and music

Audio effects add more depth to every game. A right sound at the right time makes everything feel more real. Imagine shooting a gun. Without the sound, it will never feel right.

Music in games is used to set the mood, similar to music in movies. A good choice of music can make a game better and vice versa. Usually, we want to use a music track that loops well.

You will find the music and sounds in the code bundle as well.

Audio file formats

There are many audio file formats available for use. For a full list, refer to the official list again at `http://developer.android.com/guide/appendix/media-formats.html`.

The most popular formats are WAV, MP3, and OGG for both sounds and music. While the WAV format supports many types of both lossy and lossless compression, the MP3 and OGG formats are lossy only. Lossy compression in audio works in a similar way to the one in graphics. The sound wave is transformed and some parts are cut off. This is why a highly compressed audio file can sound like speaking from a bad phone.

The OGG file format is recommended because it has easily adjustable quality settings and produces slightly smaller files than the MP3 format.

Sound effects

For our game, we only need the jumping sound and the sound of falling when the game is over. We could, of course, add more sounds, but this will be enough to illustrate the sound handling in AndEngine.

There are a few good websites that allow users to search for sounds by name, tags, and licenses. We are going to use CC-0 licensed audio files. The sounds used in the game can be found at `http://www.freesound.org/`.

For the jumping sound, you can use almost anything. A short tap or a bottle being opened will do. The falling sound in our game is the same sound they use in cartoons, made by a whistle.

Music

Getting the right music might be difficult. CC-0 music is not very common. However, for the purpose of this book, we can again use Open Game Art Bundle. We only need one track that will play during the game and loop indefinitely.

 Many games will work well without music as well. Don't get stuck on looking for the right track.

Scene diagram

A scene diagram is useful when designing the skeleton of the application. For now, the **scene** is just a screen that is part of our game. We want to have a few different screens in our game, that is, different scenes. A typical game contains at least a splash scene, a menu scene, and a game scene. A splash scene is usually used to load resources in the background while showing a badge or logo of the game author.

We can add a loading scene between the menu and the game or between different levels or stages of the game. Some games will also have a special scene for game settings, final score, hall of fame, and so on.

We will keep our scenes to a minimum. The following is a simple diagram that shows transitions from one scene to another. Notice the **Back** label. That means the user taps the back button on the device.

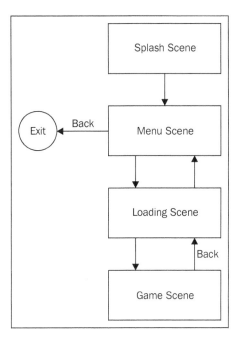

The splash and loading scenes are very simple and we do not need to spend time designing them right now. We could design our menu scene, but it won't benefit us much at this point. Let's start coding.

Summary

Concept is an important part in making a game. Not only do you get an idea of how your game is going to look, but it will also show you most of the resources that you are going to need. It's also important to think your idea through before coding and identify any possible caveats. Later, when you start coding and get stuck, get back to your concept.

In this chapter, we have drafted our game and its rules. We have also designed our game screen using the real assets that we are going to use in our game. The concept will serve as the blueprint to our game.

In the next chapter, we will load the assets to memory in order to use them. We will list the different ways of loading the graphics and types of textures. We are going to see the most common unwanted artifacts that can appear in AndEngine games, and we will discuss how to prevent them. Finally, we are going to use the assets to create our main character and add it to the game.

From Assets to Entities

3

We have our draft and it's time to convert the ideas into reality. In the first part of this chapter, we are going to see how assets—images, fonts, sounds, and music—are loaded into the memory. We will go through different ways of loading images based on the desired quality and performance. This chapter will also point out the most common mistakes made when storing and using textures.

In the second part, we will create the entities that will be used throughout the game. This is an important transition from a static image to an interactive object.

Managing resources

In many games written in AndEngine, you will see the `ResourceManager` class. It's one of the established patterns that you should be using as well. `ResourceManager` is simply a class that takes care of loading and unloading of the resources. Because the memory in Android devices is very limited, it is important to have a centralized point that will ensure each asset is loaded only once and made available throughout the entire game code. When working with limited space, you can also consider unloading resources that are not being currently used.

> When you suspend a game by pressing the Home button or when another activity takes over, for example, when receiving a call, resources might be unloaded automatically. AndEngine makes them available again when the control is returned to the game.

The `ResourceManager` class is usually designed as a **singleton**. That is another design pattern. It ensures that only one instance of the class is created during the entire run of the program. We will make this one instance available through a static method called `getInstance()`.

Let's start by creating a barebone Resource Manager. This can be done as follows:

```
package is.kul.learningandengine;

public class ResourceManager {
  // single instance is created only
  private static final ResourceManager INSTANCE = new
    ResourceManager();

  // constructor is private to ensure nobody can call it from
    outside
  private ResourceManager() { }

  public static ResourceManager getInstance() {
    return INSTANCE;
  }
}
```

Because the Resource Manager will be available from any place in the code, we can make use of it and put some commonly used objects here. Add the following two snippets into the code of the ResourceManager class. First, declare the common objects, as follows:

```
//common objects
public GameActivity activity;
public Engine engine;
public Camera camera;
public VertexBufferObjectManager vbom;
```

Then, add a method to create the Resource Manager, as follows:

```
public void create(GameActivity activity, Engine engine, Camera
  camera, VertexBufferObjectManager vbom) {
  this.activity = activity;
  this.engine = engine;
  this.camera = camera;
  this.vbom = vbom;
}
```

The objects we are going to use are as follows:

* activity: This is our game activity. The activity classes extend the Context class. The Context class holds a lot of important information and provides useful methods. We will make use of some of the activity classes later.

- `engine`: Sometimes, we need to manipulate the engine itself. The `engine` instance is available from the `activity` class as well, but this way it's easier to use it.

- `camera`: Similar to the `engine` field, we sometimes need a handle to the `camera` object.

- `vbom`: **Vertex Buffer Object** (**VBO**) is used to upload vertex data (points with position, color, normal vector, and so on) to the video memory. In OpenGL, almost everything is rendered using vertex data. VBO resides in the video memory and that makes rendering it faster. Vertex Buffer Object manager is a manager of these objects. It simplifies the use of VBOs in the game, and we will use it often.

Loading graphics

We will start by loading the graphics. First, let's go through some basic terms:

- **Texture**: From *texture mapping*, texture is a surface applied to a 3D object. In a 2D world, the 3D object is usually a rectangle (a quad is made up of two triangles) viewed in orthographic projection.

- **Texture atlas**: This is a collection of textures (subimages) on a single image. We can imagine it as a page in a photo album with small pictures and stickers placed on the page.

- **Texture region**: This is the definition of the texture in a texture atlas.

In AndEngine and Android in general, we are making use of texture atlases because they limit the amount of operations needed to load and unload images from the video memory.

In our game, we are going to use the following texture regions in a single atlas. Let's add the following code to the `ResourceManager` class:

```
//game textures
public ITiledTextureRegion playerTextureRegion;
public ITiledTextureRegion enemyTextureRegion;
public ITextureRegion platformTextureRegion;
public ITextureRegion cloud1TextureRegion;
public ITextureRegion cloud2TextureRegion;

private BuildableBitmapTextureAtlas gameTextureAtlas;
```

We have defined the five texture regions. Notice that two of the regions are **tiled texture regions**. They are in fact the same as the texture regions, but they define subregions within themselves. This is useful for sprites that change shape or are animated.

The following figure shows what an example texture atlas looks like. The regions are numbered from one to five. Regions one and five are the tiled regions. The backgrounds are used only for illustration.

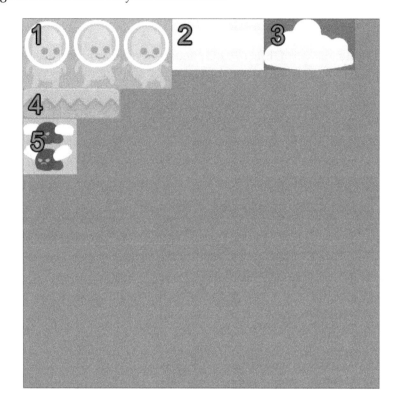

We are going to use a buildable texture atlas. When placing the images onto a texture atlas, you can either specify the positions manually, use some external software to create the atlas for you, or use AndEngine's built-in facility to create the atlas automatically. For our purpose, automatic creation is the best. It will result in a similar texture atlas to the preceding example.

We will expect all of our assets from the previous chapter to be located in the `assets/gfx` directory.

Add the following method to the `ResourceManager` class:

```
public void loadGameGraphics() {
  BitmapTextureAtlasTextureRegionFactory.setAssetBasePath("gfx/");
  gameTextureAtlas = new BuildableBitmapTextureAtlas(activity.
    getTextureManager(),
```

```
      1024, 512, BitmapTextureFormat.RGBA_8888, TextureOptions.
      BILINEAR_PREMULTIPLYALPHA);

   playerTextureRegion = BitmapTextureAtlasTextureRegionFactory.
      createTiledFromAsset(
      gameTextureAtlas, activity.getAssets(), "player.png", 3, 1);

   enemyTextureRegion = BitmapTextureAtlasTextureRegionFactory.
      createTiledFromAsset(
      gameTextureAtlas, activity.getAssets(), "enemy.png", 1, 2);

   platformTextureRegion = BitmapTextureAtlasTextureRegionFactory.
      createFromAsset(
      gameTextureAtlas, activity.getAssets(), "platform.png");

   cloud1TextureRegion = BitmapTextureAtlasTextureRegionFactory.
      createFromAsset(
      gameTextureAtlas, activity.getAssets(), "cloud1.png");

   cloud2TextureRegion = BitmapTextureAtlasTextureRegionFactory.
      createFromAsset(
      gameTextureAtlas, activity.getAssets(), "cloud2.png");

   try {
      gameTextureAtlas.build(new
         BlackPawnTextureAtlasBuilder<IBitmapTextureAtlasSource,
         BitmapTextureAtlas>(2, 0, 2));
      gameTextureAtlas.load();

   } catch (final TextureAtlasBuilderException e) {
      throw new RuntimeException("Error while loading game
         textures", e);
   }
}
```

The first line sets the current working directory for the texture to assets/gfx. Then, the bitmap texture atlas is initialized. As mentioned earlier, we could create either a simple bitmap texture atlas or a buildable bitmap texture atlas. To make things easier for us, we use the buildable option and let the algorithm place our textures automatically. The only thing you need to take care of is the size of the atlas. It must be big enough to fit all the regions.

Bitmap texture format

The bitmap texture format specifies the color resolution and quality of the texture. There are currently three formats implemented, which are as follows:

- **RGBA_8888**: This has 32-bit textures and the highest quality. It stores alpha channel (transparency).

- **RGBA_4444**: This has 16-bit textures with an alpha channel. You will experience quality loss; colors are matched using the nearest equivalent. It can create unwanted artifacts, but saves a lot of memory.

- **RGB_565**: This has 16-bit textures without an alpha channel; green channel has more bits, because it's most important for the human eye.

Texture options

Texture options is another setting that influences quality. There are eight options in total and they are a combination of three flags: interpolation, alpha channel settings, and repeating. The possible constants are as follows:

- `NEAREST`

- `BILINEAR`

- `REPEATING_NEAREST`

- `REPEATING_BILINEAR`

- `NEAREST_PREMULTIPLYALPHA`

- `BILINEAR_PREMULTIPLYALPHA`

- `REPEATING_NEAREST_PREMULTIPLYALPHA`

- `REPEATING_BILINEAR_PREMULTIPLYALPHA`

 If you don't specify the `TextureOptions` parameter, the default setting is used. Here, the `DEFAULT` value is `NEAREST`.

Interpolation

When resizing the images, the interpolation option specifies how the image is resampled (shrunk or enlarged).

Nearest-neighbor interpolation

Nearest neighbor uses a technique where the final pixel in the target image is calculated from the nearest pixel in the source image.

The following screenshots are examples of what it looks like when you enlarge or shrink an image using the nearest-neighbor interpolation:

Original

The following enlarged image looks pixelated. The image has not been resized smoothly.

Enlarged

The following image that has been shrunk has lost some of its details, which is expected, but notice the left wing. It looks very different from the original.

Shrunk

Here's the reason. When resizing images, first the position in the original image is calculated and then the nearest pixel to that point is used. This is described in the following figure:

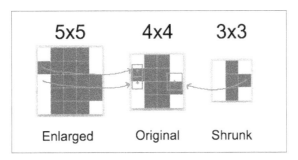

This interpolation is not very precise, but it preserves the hard edges. It is, however, very seldom used in games on the Android platform, because resizing happens a lot due to the number of different resolutions. You would see a lot of unwanted artifacts when using this interpolation. On the other hand, this interpolation is very fast.

Bilinear interpolation

Imagine you have two discrete values and you want to know the value somewhere between them. **Linear interpolation** is one of the ways to fill the holes between the points. **Bilinear interpolation** is an extension of linear interpolation into 2D. The resampled images can look blurry. See the following screenshot:

Original

The following enlarged image has been smoothly resized. It's a bit blurry, but not pixelated.

Enlarged

The image that has been shrunk lost some of its details, which is expected, but the shapes are almost the same as in the original.

Shrunk

Imagine that instead of measuring which is the nearest pixel to the target pixel in the source grid, we will project all four corners and then calculate the result from these four values. This is described in the following figure. The bilinear interpolation is slower, but with the current graphics hardware, you won't notice any slowdown.

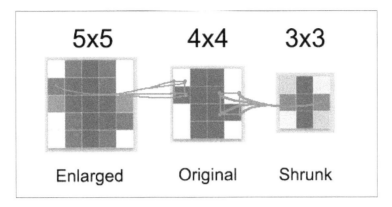

Repeating

Repeating is very simple. In the nonrepeating case, if you resize the texture, the image will be stretched or shrunk. In the repeating case, it will stay the same size and it will repeat as necessary. This type of texture is typically used to draw a wall or a floor. The following figure has been scaled to 250 percent using the repeating settings. Notice that the texture repeats 2.5 times in both directions.

Alpha channel settings

There are two modes for alpha: straight alpha and premultiplied alpha. When handled correctly, these two are equal. The difference is that in the premultiplied mode, the color is matted, usually by black color, according to the alpha value.

For example, a blue pixel with 50 percent alpha in the straight alpha texture will have RGBA: [0, 0, 255, 127] value. The same pixel in the premultiplied version will have RGBA: [0, 0, 127, 127] value.

Creating the regions

We use the BitmapTextureAtlasTextureRegionFactory class to create texture regions. You can create regions from assets (the images in the assets directory), resources (Android resources in the res directory), or any source object that produces bitmaps. We are going to use the first option. Notice that we are creating both simple and tiled assets. We simply specify which texture atlas to use and which file to load. The extra two parameters in tiled assets are the number of columns and rows. Consider the following code:

```
...
gameTextureAtlas = new BuildableBitmapTextureAtlas
  (activity.getTextureManager(),
  1024, 512, BitmapTextureFormat.RGBA_8888,
  TextureOptions.BILINEAR_PREMULTIPLYALPHA);

playerTextureRegion = BitmapTextureAtlasTextureRegionFactory.
  createTiledFromAsset(
  gameTextureAtlas, activity.getAssets(), "player.png", 3, 1);

enemyTextureRegion = BitmapTextureAtlasTextureRegionFactory.
  createTiledFromAsset(
  gameTextureAtlas, activity.getAssets(), "enemy.png", 1, 2);

platformTextureRegion = BitmapTextureAtlasTextureRegionFactory.
  createFromAsset(
    gameTextureAtlas, activity.getAssets(), "platform.png");
...
```

Because we are using a buildable bitmap texture atlas, we do not have to specify where to place the region in the atlas. If we use the simple atlas, we would have to call another method that has two extra parameters, which are the x and y positions of the region within the atlas.

Building the atlas

Finally, the code in the try and catch code blocks builds the atlas. In other words, it calls the algorithm (called BlackPawn) to place the regions on the atlas. This is shown in the following code:

```
try {
  gameTextureAtlas.build(new
    BlackPawnTextureAtlasBuilder<IBitmapTextureAtlasSource,
    BitmapTextureAtlas>(2, 0, 2));
  gameTextureAtlas.load();
```

```
    } catch (final TextureAtlasBuilderException e) {
      throw new RuntimeException("Error while loading game textures"
        , e);
    }
```

We are catching the `TextureAtlasBuilderException` that can happen when it is not possible to place all regions on the atlas. In this case, our application will end with an error.

The `BlackPawn` builder has the following three parameters:

- **Atlas border spacing**: This is the minimum distance between the atlas border and the texture border
- **Source spacing**: This is the space between the texture regions
- **Source padding**: This is the extra space inside the region's border

These parameters are used to prevent unwanted artifacts around sprites. These are caused by texture and alpha bleeding.

Texture and alpha bleeding

The two main issues when creating sprites from textures in texture regions are **texture** and **alpha bleeding**. They can appear any time, but mostly they create lines around sprites that are visible usually when playing in a different resolution than the one the game was designed for.

Texture bleeding

The following figure shows what texture bleeding looks like. Notice the two black lines at the top of the sprite.

The sprite was sampled from the tiled texture region in the following figure. The border shows the area that was used for sampling. It goes beyond the limit of the single tile, because of the interpolation. The pixels at the border of the lower tile are calculated using the last row of pixels in the upper tile.

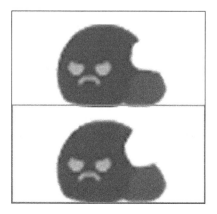

This can happen due to two reasons. First, we have a tiled sprite without spacing (or padding) between the tiles. Then we can see these lines, which are parts of the other tile. Secondly, when placing these regions onto the atlas, we place them too close to each other and a region (tiled or not) will sample some values from the neighboring regions.

The former can only be prevented when creating the tiled spritesheets. Make sure you leave some space around the borders of the sprites. The latter can be prevented by placing the regions onto the atlas while leaving some borders around them (padding or spacing). This is what the `BlackPawn` texture builder algorithm parameters are for.

Alpha bleeding

Alpha bleeding is caused when resampling images with alpha channel. It is not as obvious as texture bleeding. When you create an image with transparency, the transparent pixels still have red, green, and blue values. Usually, they are set to black or white. When sampling the pixels on the border, sometimes these are sampled to calculate the final color. Alpha bleeding can sometimes be prevented in AndEngine using the premultiplied alpha variants of textures. But in most cases, it won't be noticeable.

The following figure is an example of what alpha bleeding looks like. The little image on the left is placed over a white background and is moved by a pixel to the right first. Alpha bleeding doesn't happen. But then, it's moved only half a pixel to the right. This can easily happen, because our game can be displayed on different resolution screens than originally planned or the sprite can be resized.

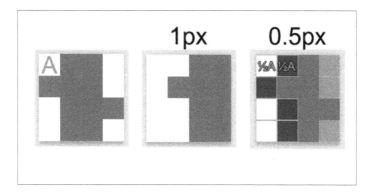

The problem here is that the graphics library needs to sample half of pixel **A**. Pixel **A** is transparent, but it's underlying color is in fact black with zero alpha. So, when a real color is needed, 50 percent black is used and this will bleed into the blue making it darker.

Unloading graphics

When working with a lot of graphics assets in your game, the memory might not fit all of them. Also, because an Android device's memory is quite limited and there can be multiple running applications at the same time, it's important to unload resources you don't need.

When a user presses the Home button, the graphics resources are unloaded automatically and are loaded back when the controls are given back to the game. Sometimes, the Android system decides that it needs all the memory occupied by the game. In that case, the game is terminated and when the user runs it again, it is started from the beginning.

When working with multiple scenes, a good practice is to unload the graphics resources that are no longer needed. To do that, you only need to call the `unload()` method of the texture atlas, as shown in the following line of code:

```
gameTextureAtlas.unload();
```

In our case, we are not going to use it because we don't need to unload any resources.

Loading sounds and music

Both sounds and music are stored in audio files. Any type of audio file that the Android media player can play can be used in AndEngine. The most popular file formats are WAV, MP3, and OGG. Using OGG is highly recommended, because it's a well-documented open format with good compression.

 You can use free software, such as Audacity, to convert between the file formats. Audacity has built-in OGG support. You can download it from `http://audacity.sourceforge.net/`.

If your sound and music files are in other formats, you can still use them. In our example, we will use OGG files.

Start by defining the fields for sounds and music. Add the following code to the `ResourceManager` class:

```
//sounds
public Sound soundFall;
public Sound soundJump;

//music
public Music music;
```

Then, add a method to load them. This is shown in the following code:

```
public void loadGameAudio() {
  try {
    SoundFactory.setAssetBasePath("sfx/");
    soundJump = SoundFactory.createSoundFromAsset
      (activity.getSoundManager(), activity, "jump.ogg");
    soundFall = SoundFactory.createSoundFromAsset
      (activity.getSoundManager(), activity, "fall.ogg");

    MusicFactory.setAssetBasePath("mfx/");
    music = MusicFactory.createMusicFromAsset
      (activity.getMusicManager(), activity, "music.ogg");
  } catch (Exception e) {
    throw new RuntimeException("Error while loading audio", e);
  }
}
```

We are using two different factories: SoundFactory and MusicFactory. They both have the setAssetBasePath method to set the root folder for sounds and music.

Loading both music and sound is pretty straightforward. Simply pass the sound or music manager to the factory, the Android context instance (that is our activity), and the path starting from the root folder that we set with the setAssetBasePath() method.

The basic difference between sound and music objects is that sounds are pooled and many sounds can be played at once. In the case of music, only one file can be played at once, and you are given more precise controls over the audio track, for example, seek, rewind, and pause. In both cases, you can set the volume or mute the audio.

Unloading sounds and music

It is possible to unload sounds and music as well by using the release() method on the sound or music object. However, audio is stored in a different memory than the graphics (textures), and we won't usually run into memory problems while using them. For simple games, it's safe to just keep them in memory.

Loading fonts

Fonts in AndEngine are stored in textures and loading fonts is similar to loading graphics. AndEngine can take a font file or it can render a system font to the texture. This means that every character will be defined as a small texture region on a big texture atlas. As a consequence, you have to create a font for a fixed size and color. You can also create a stroke around the font.

Use contrasting colors such as white and black to create a font with a stroke. It helps the readability of the text.

Also, you must define a texture big enough to fit all the characters you are going to need. AndEngine creates the characters one by one and puts them on the texture as they are requested.

We are going to use only one font. If more sizes are needed, text can be scaled, but it's recommended to create separate fonts for separate sizes. Creating the font in white allows us to change its color later. If we create the font in black, the color can't be changed anymore.

Add the following code to the `ResourceManager` class:

```
//font
public Font font;

public void loadFont() {
    font = FontFactory.createStroke(activity.getFontManager(),
        activity.getTextureManager(), 256, 256,
        Typeface.create(Typeface.SANS_SERIF, Typeface.BOLD), 50,
        true, Color.WHITE_ABGR_PACKED_INT, 2,
        Color.BLACK_ABGR_PACKED_INT);
    font.load();
}
```

The `FontFactory` class has methods to create fonts and stroked fonts from a system font and from font files. In our example, we create a stroked font.

The texture size we are using is 256 x 256 pixels big and the font size is 50 px. This won't fit all the characters in the font, but it's big enough for our case. It is possible to use the `font.prepareLetters();` method to create the characters you will need in the texture beforehand. If you end up with black boxes instead of characters, you will know that your texture is too small.

We are creating a bold Sans Serif system font of size 50, which roughly translates to 50 pixel-tall characters (maximum) with variable width.

The Boolean parameter we are using (`true`) means we want the font to be anti-aliased (smooth edges).

The color is passed as a **packed integer**. We don't need to worry about how it is calculated because AndEngine's `Color` class can convert it for us from separate red, green, blue, and alpha values. Some common values such as black and white are already precalculated.

Unloading fonts

Because fonts are nothing else but textures, you can unload them the same way. Simply call the following function:

```
font.unload();
```

Putting it all together

When we have created all the necessary methods in the `ResourceManager` class, we also need to call them at the right time. Let's go back to the `GameActivity` class and change the following method:

```
@Override
public void onCreateResources(
  OnCreateResourcesCallback pOnCreateResourcesCallback)
  throws IOException {
  ResourceManager.getInstance().create(this, getEngine(),
    getEngine().getCamera(), getVertexBufferObjectManager());
  ResourceManager.getInstance().loadFont();
  ResourceManager.getInstance().loadGameAudio();
  ResourceManager.getInstance().loadGameGraphics();
  pOnCreateResourcesCallback.onCreateResourcesFinished();
}
```

First, we instantiate our singleton Resource Manager. We pass all the important objects in order to store the references in Resource Manager. Then we load the font, audio, and graphics, and finally call the `callback` method to indicate we are done loading resources.

> If you load a resource twice without unloading it, two copies will be created in the memory. This is called a memory leak. If you repeat it several times, the game will either crash or the user will experience glitches.

We have finished loading all the resources we will need for now, and we can move on to creating entities that will be displayed on the screen.

Entities

Everything you can display in AndEngine is an entity. The `Entity` class is a basic class that stands on top of the hierarchy. The `Entity` class has all the parameters the displayable objects need, such as position, scale factor, color, and so on. But on its own, it doesn't display anything.

The `Entity` class can also have children, both in Java class hierarchy and in the hierarchy of AndEngine objects.

For the former case, let's take the `Sprite` class as an example. A sprite in AndEngine is a simple image rendered on a quad (a square made of two triangles). The `Sprite` class extends the `Shape` class, which already knows what to do when the programmer sets its height and width; therefore, the `Sprite` class doesn't need to implement it. Also, the `Shape` class extends the `Entity` class. See the following diagram for another example:

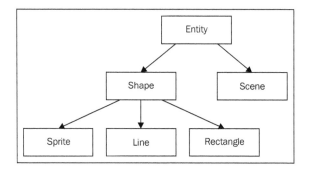

The latter case means that you can attach one entity to another. It doesn't matter what type it is, whether it's a sprite, shape, or anything else, as long as it is an entity. The most basic example of this behavior is a scene and its children.

Scene

AndEngine can display one scene at a time. The `Scene` object is passed to the engine. A scene is an entity too. A scene can have any number of entities attached to it. It can also have a child scene. This is useful when you want to quickly show, for example, a pop up at the end of a level. The hierarchy of attached entities will look similar to what is shown in the following diagram:

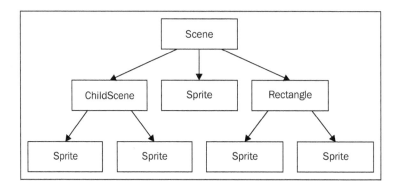

Notice that a sprite can be attached to a rectangle. Also, a rectangle can be attached to a sprite, because both the objects are extending the `Entity` class.

We will start by creating a scene. For now, we only want to have one scene, the GameScene. But later, we might want to add another scene for menu or even more scenes. It's a very good practice to think about what all our scenes have in common and then create a common ancestor for all our scenes.

 Use Java packages to organize classes. Put all scene classes in to a subpackage scene. In our case, that will be a package called is.kul.learningandengine.scene.

AbstractScene

The AbstractScene class serves as a base for all other scenes. It's like a template for creating scenes. It's also designed as an abstract class, which means we can't create an instance of AbstractScene. Abstract classes are typically used when we want to define some default behavior in child classes. We define this behavior in regular methods of the abstract class and we force the child classes to implement the other methods by marking them as abstract.

The following code describes what the Java class looks like:

```java
package is.kul.learningandengine.scene;

public abstract class AbstractScene extends Scene {
  protected ResourceManager res = ResourceManager.getInstance();

  protected Engine engine = res.engine;
  protected GameActivity activity = res.activity;
  protected VertexBufferObjectManager vbom = res.vbom;
  protected Camera camera = res.camera;

  public abstract void populate();

  public void destroy() {
  }

  public void onBackKeyPressed() {
    Debug.d("Back key pressed");
  }

  public abstract void onPause();

  public abstract void onResume();
}
```

The basic fields are added and populated from the `ResourceManager` class. This is just a convenience so we can directly access them in every scene.

The abstract method `populate()` must be implemented in the scenes that extend `AbstractScene`.

The `destroy()` method is not abstract and has a default behavior to do nothing. Sometimes, we need to do something when the scene is destroyed. In that case, we can override this method.

The `onBackKeyPressed()` method is called when the players press the back key on their phone. Each scene should behave differently. For example, you could go back to the menu scene from the game scene, and you should exit the game from the menu scene when the back key is pressed.

The last two methods define actions to be taken when the game is paused and resumed. This can happen when the user presses the Home button, or it can be triggered by an incoming call and so on.

GameScene

In a typical multiscene game, we need to have another class, `SceneManager`, that will take care of switching the scenes and handle the pause, resume, and back key press. But we are going to start with a single scene. This will allow us to quickly develop the game itself first and only later add other scenes.

Create a class called `GameScene` in the `is.kul.learningandengine.scene` package and make it extend `AbstractScene`. It should look like the following code snippet:

```
package is.kul.learningandengine.scene;

public class GameScene extends AbstractScene {

  @Override
  public void populate() {

  }

  @Override
  public void onPause() {

  }
```

```
@Override
public void onResume() {

    }

}
```

Now, let's go back to the `GameActivity` class and make it create our `GameScene` class. Change the following two methods:

```
@Override
public void onCreateScene(OnCreateSceneCallback
  pOnCreateSceneCallback)
  throws IOException {
  Scene scene = new GameScene();
  pOnCreateSceneCallback.onCreateSceneFinished(scene);
}

@Override
public void onPopulateScene(Scene pScene,
  OnPopulateSceneCallback pOnPopulateSceneCallback)
  throws IOException {
  AbstractScene scene = (AbstractScene) pScene;
  scene.populate();
  pOnPopulateSceneCallback.onPopulateSceneFinished();
}
```

Let's add something to the scene and test whether we have done everything correctly.

Background

Each scene has a background. The background is always drawn first, therefore, it will always be displayed behind all other entities as expected. There are many kinds of backgrounds. They are as follows:

- `EntityBackground`: This is the simplest class; any entity can be a background.
- `SpriteBackground`: This is a single sprite background.
- `RepeatingSpriteBackground`: This is a tiled background; a single sprite is repeated to cover the whole background.
- `ParallaxBackground`: This is a background that creates a feeling of depth by using several layers that move with different velocities.
- `AutoParallaxBackground`: This is the same as `ParallaxBackground` but moves on its own. This is useful for creating effects with moving clouds and so on.

Let's create the same background as the one in the game concept explained in *Chapter 2, Game Concept and Assets*. We will simply set the background to light blue color and add two clouds. The easiest way to do this is to use `EntityBackground`. Change the `populate()` method in the `GameScene` class as follows:

```
@Override
public void populate() {
  createBackground();
}

private void createBackground() {
  Entity background = new Entity();
  Sprite cloud1 = new Sprite(200, 300, res.cloud1TextureRegion,
    vbom);
  Sprite cloud2 = new Sprite(300, 600, res.cloud2TextureRegion,
    vbom);
  background.attachChild(cloud1);
  background.attachChild(cloud2);
  setBackground(new EntityBackground(0.82f, 0.96f, 0.97f,
    background));
}
```

The preceding code creates a new entity and attaches two entities to it. Then, it creates a new `EntityBackground` class and sets it as the game scene's background. Notice that the background color is passed in the constructor. This is because the entity itself has color, but doesn't know how to render it. `EntityBackground` solves that problem.

If you try running the game now, you will notice that the clouds have noticeable bandings — color stripes instead of a smooth gradient. This is because AndEngine uses 16-bit rendering by default. There are several ways to improve the quality.

First, you can enable **dithering**. This means that the 32-bit colors will be created by using small dots of 16-bit colors. Because the screen resolution is big, usually it won't be noticeable. Just add the following line to the `onCreateEngineOptions` method in the `GameActivity` class:

```
engineOptions.getRenderOptions().setDithering(true);
```

The other option is to force 32-bit rendering. This can be done by setting the bit size parameters for each color, as shown in the following code snippet:

```
engineOptions.getRenderOptions().getConfigChooserOptions().
  setRequestedAlphaSize(8);
engineOptions.getRenderOptions().getConfigChooserOptions().
  setRequestedRedSize(8);
```

```
engineOptions.getRenderOptions().getConfigChooserOptions().
   setRequestedGreenSize(8);
engineOptions.getRenderOptions().getConfigChooserOptions().
   setRequestedBlueSize(8);
```

We are going to use dithering. See the following figures as a comparison for the differences between 32-bit rendering, 16-bit rendering, and 16-bit with dithering. The colors were enhanced to illustrate the differences.

 On a small screen, the differences are much less noticeable.

The following figure was rendered in 32-bits. Each line of pixels has its own color. This is how the image was originally drawn.

32-bit rendering

The following figure shows what happens when we use 16-bit rendering without dithering. Two or three lines of pixels now share the same color value. While there are about 16 million colors with 256 different alpha values in a 32-bit space, there are only 65,536 colors in 16-bit space without using alpha and just 4,096 when using alpha.

16-bit rendering

The previous screenshot shows the effect of dithering. When rendering in very fine resolution, the human eye can't differentiate individual pixels anymore and will perceive two pixels of different colors as a single area of another color. Have a look at the following figure:

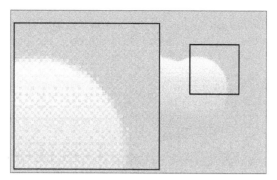

Enlarged figure of 16-bit with dithering

Sprite, tiled sprite, and animated sprite

In the preceding background example, we created two sprites. A sprite is a single piece of graphic that can be put on the screen and manipulated. In AndEngine, it's an entity that knows how to take a texture region and render it on the screen.

A tiled sprite is just a sprite that has more than one shape (more than one texture region). It has a method to switch between the tiles, called the setCurrentTileIndex method.

An animated sprite is the same as the tiled sprite, but it has a feature to automatically switch from one tile to another creating an animation. See the animate method.

For simple objects that are created once and put on the screen, simply using the Sprite, TiledSprite, or AnimatedSprite classes is good enough, such as in our background example. But when creating more sprites that are heavily customized, it's highly recommended to create a custom class extending the Sprite class and a factory class that will create the entity with preset parameters. We are going to make use of the factory pattern for our entities.

The factory pattern is typically used when we have an entity and especially multiple instances of that entity with some defined behavior, but we don't care about how it is created. The creation of the entity might be difficult and include many steps. Instead of putting the code in the entity itself (very bad) or putting the code somewhere in the scene code (less bad), we create another class. Its single purpose is to create the entity.

It's like a real factory, let's say a factory that makes rubber ducks. We want our duck to quack when squeezed. But we don't care how the duck is manufactured as long as it quacks. So, our duck factory is like a supplier of ducks. Also if we need to, we can change the supplier without modifying anything else.

It's the same with our code. We will have a factory for the player and we don't care how it is created. If we need, we can change the class to create the player in a different way without changing any other code in the game.

Main character

For our main character, we will need two classes: the `Player` class and the `PlayerFactory` class. We are separating the functionality based on a simple rule of thumb: each class should have a single responsibility. When we start adding more functionality, the separation will make it much easier.

Player class

We start by extending the `TiledSprite` class in the `is.kul.learningandengine.entity` package, as follows:

```
package is.kul.learningandengine.entity;

import org.andengine.entity.sprite.TiledSprite;
import org.andengine.opengl.texture.region.ITiledTextureRegion;
import org.andengine.opengl.vbo.VertexBufferObjectManager;

public class Player extends TiledSprite {

  boolean dead = false;

  public Player(float pX, float pY,
    ITiledTextureRegion pTiledTextureRegion,
    VertexBufferObjectManager pVertexBufferObjectManager) {
    super(pX, pY, pTiledTextureRegion,
      pVertexBufferObjectManager);
  }

  public boolean isDead() {
```

```
      return dead;
    }

    public void setDead(boolean dead) {
      this.dead = dead;
    }

    public void turnLeft() {
      setFlippedHorizontal(true);
    }

    public void turnRight() {
      setFlippedHorizontal(false);
    }

    public void fly() {
      setCurrentTileIndex(0);
    }

    public void fall() {
      setCurrentTileIndex(1);
    }

    public void die() {
      setDead(true);
    setCurrentTileIndex(2);
    }
  }
```

When extending any `Sprite` class, we need to implement at least one constructor. We've added a Boolean field indicating that the player is dead, which we can use later. We've also added a few convenience methods that call the `TiledSprite` methods. We just give them meaningful names.

The `Player` class expects it will be created with a tiled sprite that has at least three tiles. Tile 0 should be the fly (jump up) shape, tile 1 should be the falling shape, and tile 2 should be the falling below the last platform shape, in other words, the end of the game.

We also use a simple trick. We flip the sprite horizontally when going left, because our images are drawn facing right.

PlayerFactory class

The `PlayerFactory` class is responsible for creating the player entity. It is a singleton class, and its code is very simple, as follows:

```
package is.kul.learningandengine.factory;

import is.kul.learningandengine.ResourceManager;
import is.kul.learningandengine.entity.Player;

import org.andengine.opengl.vbo.VertexBufferObjectManager;

public class PlayerFactory {
  private static PlayerFactory INSTANCE = new PlayerFactory();
  private VertexBufferObjectManager vbom;

  private PlayerFactory() {
  }

  public static PlayerFactory getInstance() {
    return INSTANCE;
  }

  public void create(VertexBufferObjectManager vbom) {
    this.vbom = vbom;
  }

  public Player createPlayer(float x, float y) {
    Player player = new Player(x, y, ResourceManager.
      getInstance().playerTextureRegion, vbom);
    player.setZIndex(2);
    return player;
  }
}
```

The only thing it does for now is create a new `Player` instance, which is the same as creating a `Sprite` instance and then setting its z-index (z-coordinate).

> AndEngine is a 2D engine, but the z-index is still used. The order of sprites added to the scene or attached to an entity defines the order in which they are drawn. If there are overlapping entities, the ones added later will be drawn *in front*. You can change this order by setting the z-index and calling the `sortChildren()` method on the parent entity. A higher z-index means the sprite is closer to the viewer.

Using the new entity and its factory

To use the factory, it must be first initialized using the `create()` method. This can be done in the constructor of the `GameScene` class, as follows:

```
public GameScene() {
   PlayerFactory.getInstance().create(vbom);
}
```

We simply create the factory while passing the Vertex Buffer Object manager to it. This will allow the factory to create drawable objects.

Next, change the `populate` method and add another method to create the player. We are going to use a field for the player, because we will need to access it throughout the entire scene code. Consider the following code:

```
private Player player;

@Override
public void populate() {
  createBackground();
  createPlayer();
}

private void createPlayer() {
  player = PlayerFactory.getInstance().createPlayer(240, 400);
  attachChild(player);
}
```

Platforms and enemies

The `Entity` and `Factory` classes for platforms and enemies are created in the same way as the `Player` classes. We are going to create them in *Chapter 5, Basic Interactions*, when we will add the physics engine to our game. In the same chapter, we will alter the player classes to work with physics.

Running the code

We have written code that is now ready to be run on an Android device. The current application will show the player's character sprite in the middle of the screen with light blue background and two clouds. You can have a look at this chapter's code in the code bundle.

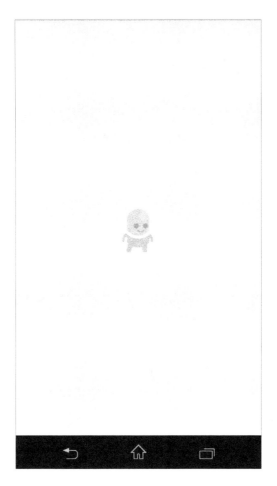

Summary

In this chapter, we have learned how to load graphics and audio files into the Android device's memory. We've seen different types of textures and the texture options that influence the quality of the displayed images. Common mistakes, texture and alpha bleeding, were described and solutions for both were provided.

We have also defined basic terms such as entity, scene, background, and sprite and two types of entity hierarchies. We have designed the basic player entity and we have learned about the factory pattern that can be used to create entities. In the end, we have put everything together to put a sprite on the screen.

In the next chapter, we will explore other basic entities, namely text and HUD. We are going to discuss the limitations of text in AndEngine in greater detail and give a basic overview about localization and national alphabets.

4
HUD and Text Display

In this chapter, we will learn about text output. We will look deeper into how fonts are created and stored and analyze the possible problems of AndEngine's way of displaying text characters. We will also learn how to create multilingual games and how to **localize** them.

We will see how to put text on a screen utilizing a **heads-up display** (HUD) in order to display the score of the game. Alternative ways of displaying text messages will also be discussed.

Finally, we will cover the basics of Android and AndEngine logging and debugging output.

Fonts and text

A font is a file that defines the characters and sometimes special glyphs and symbols that can be printed on the screen. Fonts are typically defined as vectors. Because AndEngine and the OpenGL library in general don't work with vectors, we must first create a raster or bitmap font. We can imagine it as printing the entire alphabet with special characters using a font of our choice on an image and cutting out the letters. Afterwards, we create words using these cut-outs.

The following code shows how we load the font in the `ResourceManager` class:

```
//font
public Font font;

public void loadFont() {
  font = FontFactory.createStroke(activity.getFontManager(),
    activity.getTextureManager(), 256, 256,
    Typeface.create(Typeface.SANS_SERIF, Typeface.BOLD), 50, true,
    Color.WHITE_ABGR_PACKED_INT, 2, Color.BLACK_ABGR_PACKED_INT);
  font.load();
}
```

The first parameter passed is the FontManager class. It's an AndEngine class that takes care of managing the fonts. The second parameter is the TextureManager class. We pass it in because, as we will see later in this chapter, the font is basically a texture onto which we print letters.

The third and fourth parameters are the font texture width and height. The texture used is a minimal texture that can hold the entire English alphabet using the given font and size. We are going to see how the size of the texture can lead to common problems with fonts in AndEngine.

The fifth parameter is the font used. In this example, we are using a built-in font that is available on every Android device. However, it can actually differ in size a little on different Android versions. The sixth parameter, 50, is the size of the font.

The next parameter tells AndEngine to use anti-aliasing to smoothen the edges of the text. It is followed by the eighth parameter, the font color. In our case, we will use white.

The last two parameters define a stroke around each letter as a two-pixels-wide black line.

When this code is called, the texture for the font is prepared. The font object is ready to be used for outputting text. However, the font texture is empty at this moment. How is that possible? Simply because AndEngine loads the letters and puts them onto the texture only when they are needed for the first time. This is called **lazy loading**.

We can force AndEngine to load all letters that we are going to use by calling the font.prepareLetters() method.

 AndEngine's lazy loading can cause a small lag each time a new letter is loaded. It's advisable to load the letters in advance at the beginning of the game.

Storing the font on a texture

Because AndEngine works with its own surface view, it can't simply output text as regular Android apps do. It must draw the text using small sprites. Each letter is in fact a sprite on its own. They are assembled into words by the Text class.

Let's see what happens when we load the Latin alphabet. We start with all uppercase letters and some special characters. The following assignment can be added to the loadFont() method in the ResourceManager class:

```
font.prepareLetters("01234567890ABCDEFGHIJKLMNOPQRSTUVWXYZ.,!?".to
    CharArray());
```

We are using the `toCharArray()` method because the `prepareLetters()` method expects an array of characters.

 You can opt to render only the characters that you are really going to use. Also, you can call the method with a sentence. Any repeating characters will be rendered only once and a space is not rendered at all. For example, in the sentence in the following line of code, only one E will be rendered on the texture:

```
font.prepareLetters("GAME OVER!".toCharArray());
```

The final texture will look something like the following screenshot. Note that the texture is 256 pixels wide and 256 pixels tall. Each character is defined as a texture region in this texture.

A texture 256 x 256 pixels large can fit all numbers, all uppercase Latin alphabet letters, a comma, a period, an exclamation mark, and a question mark.

 If we try to load more characters than the texture can fit, the game will crash. In reality, we would define a bigger texture.

Storing special characters and international alphabets

There are a few prerequisites for using special characters and international alphabets. First, the font used must contain them. The Android system font contains most of the UTF characters. However, some custom fonts don't. Second, AndEngine treats all letters as sprites; boxed entities, written from left to right. Any other writing systems that compile the words in a different way are not supported.

All this is very important to take into account when localizing games to other languages. Let's discuss what happens when using different international alphabets.

Characters from European languages

Most of the European language alphabets contain characters with a diacritic. They are rendered just fine, but they usually take more space. They must be rendered as separate characters and also the characters are usually taller.

First, we preload some of the characters to the texture map as follows:

```
font.prepareLetters("01234567890ABCDEFGHIJKLMNOPQRSTUVWXYZ
    ÁÉ".toCharArray());
```

The result is shown in the following screenshot:

The letters with diacritic take more space vertically. AndEngine will take care of the right positioning. Both top and bottom diacritics are rendered correctly.

Also notice that the width of each letter is different. The two new letters are the same width as the four punctuation marks combined.

Korean, Chinese, Japanese, and other similar writing systems

Generally, writing systems that contain separate characters can be rendered.

The Korean alphabet, Hangul, is in fact a syllabary. Each character is constructed from vowel and consonant parts. To render Hangul in AndEngine, you have to prepare each combination separately. This can make the texture pretty big, but it still works.

The same is true for the Japanese alphabet. Each character of both hiragana and katakana (Japanese syllabic writing system) must be rendered separately, even the characters with Japanese diacritic dakuten (double dot or circle). This can be changed by overriding the Text class and adding a special rule. But, this override is not implemented in AndEngine itself.

Finally, Chinese characters and Japanese Kanji (adopted Chinese characters) can be rendered easily. But, there are many of them. A larger texture might be needed.

Let's change the code to include the characters we would like to render. This can be done as follows:

```
font.prepareLetters("한글中文ひらがなカタカナ".toCharArray());
```

The following screenshot shows these Korean, Chinese, and Japanese characters rendered on to a texture:

If you can read Japanese, maybe you have noticed that the katakana part is composed only of *ka*, *ta*, and *na*, and one *ka* is missing. Each character is rendered only once, therefore the character *ka* is rendered only once.

Other writing systems

AndEngine has a problem rendering other writing systems. For example, Thai script, Arabic script, or the script used to write the Hindi language can't be rendered correctly. It is possible to implement a custom rendering, but it would take quite a lot of work.

Let's try to prepare some Hindi, Thai, and Arabic alphabet with this code:

```
font.prepareLetters("देवनागरीตัวอักษร· أَبْجَدِيَّة · غَرَبِينَة".toCharArray());¶
```

The following screenshot shows the result. Notice that there are some extra characters rendered separately and in general, it doesn't look like the text in the preceding line of code. This is due to the fact that some writing systems work very differently from the Latin alphabet, and AndEngine doesn't support them at all.

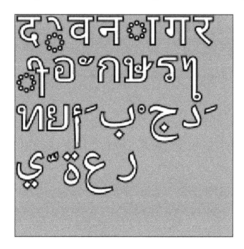

Workaround for unsupported languages

It is always possible to pre-render the text using other graphics software and use it as sprites when needed. This might not be an option in text-heavy games, but the only other option is to create a custom rendering for writing systems that are not supported.

Other limitations of the font texture

Another thing to watch out for is the size of the font. The font is rendered only once in the size specified when creating the `font` object. If you want to use fonts of different sizes, you can either scale the `Text` entity or create multiple `font` objects in different sizes.

Writing text

Now that we have our font loaded, we can use the `Text` class to print it to the screen. The `Text` class is nothing more than an entity that can assemble words and sentences from small one-letter sprites.

Adding text to the scene is very straightforward. Add a new `private` field for the score text and change the `populate()` method of the `GameScene` class as follows:

```
private Text scoreText;

@Override
public void populate() {
  createBackground();
  createPlayer();

  scoreText = new Text(16, 784, res.font, "0123456789", new
    TextOptions(HorizontalAlign.LEFT), vbom);
  scoreText.setAnchorCenter(0, 1);
  attachChild(scoreText);
}
```

This will add the text **01234567890** to the top-left corner, at the position (16, 784) of the screen. The `Text` class allows you to specify the horizontal alignment of the text with the three obvious choices: left, center, and right. If we have not used the `prepareLetters()` method before, this constructor would create the letters for us too.

We are using a new method called `setAnchorCenter()` here. When you attach an entity to another entity (or scene) at position (x, y), it is the center of the entity that gets attached at (x, y). The point of attachment of the attached entity is called the anchor center. You can change it using the aforementioned `setAnchorCenter()` method. The method takes two parameters, x and y. It's a relative position of the anchor to the entity. An anchor center at (0, 0) means bottom-left corner and (1, 1) is the top-right corner. The center of the entity is (0.5, 0.5), which is the default position.

The following illustration shows how the anchor center affects the placement. The blue circle is the anchor center and the exact position of the anchor center is written in black. When we place the rectangle in the center of the scene, the two cases will be different. The green circle indicates the center of the scene.

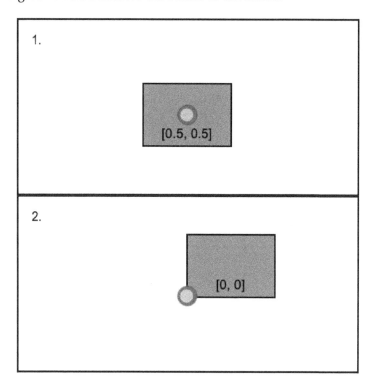

We have set the anchor center to the top-left corner. This is beneficial because we want to fit the text in the top-left corner of the scene.

You can always change the text by calling the method setText() from the Text class, as shown in the following line of code:

```
scoreText.setText("NO SCORE");
```

This also generates any characters that haven't been generated before; this can cause AndEngine to lag.

To change the size or the color of the text, we can use the setScale() and setColor() methods that are available for all classes extending the Entity class.

The following screenshot shows how the scene looks with the attached text:

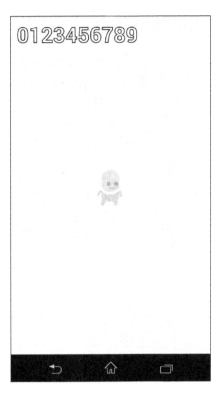

But what will happen when the camera moves to another place? So far, we have only worked with a static scene. Of course, in a real game, we want the camera to follow the main character as it jumps up. If we attach the text to the scene, then the text disappears as soon as the character moves up far enough to pass the text.

Attaching text to the scene is useful if the text is actually part of the scene, for example, like writing on a wall. But for score text, we want the text to be independent of camera movement. That's why we need HUD.

HUD

To understand how heads-up display works, simply imagine that we draw something on a piece of glass and put this glass in front of a camera in a way that whenever the camera moves, the glass moves with it. This is exactly what we need to display the score.

AndEngine has a concept of **camera scene**, a scene that works as the glass. HUD is a special camera scene that has no background, so it is always see-through.

Have a look at the following illustration of how the HUD works. The black rectangle defines the visible portion of the scene. The HUD is the translucent rectangle. The resulting image has the text in the top-left corner. Even if the visible portion of the scene changes because of camera movement, the text will stay in the corner.

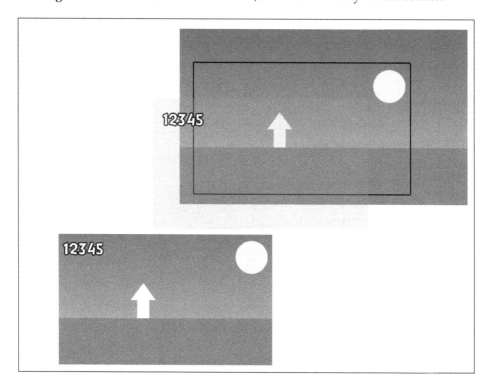

Another important feature of the HUD is that it is always drawn last. Even if we set a z-index of an entity to a lower number in the HUD than all the other entities in the scene, the HUD entity will be drawn on top of them. An entity attached to the HUD can only be covered by another entity in the HUD.

There is always only one HUD per camera. Also, a common mistake is to attach the HUD to the scene. It is possible, because in the end, the HUD is just an entity too. But in that case, we would lose all the advantages of the HUD. The correct way to use HUD is to set the HUD parameter of the camera using the following method:

```
HUD hud = new HUD();
camera.setHUD(hud);
```

Let's modify the code from the *Writing Text* section, where we added text and attached it to the scene. Now, we will create an HUD and attach the text to it. Change the `GameScene` class as follows:

```
private Text scoreText;

@Override
public void populate() {
  createBackground();
  createPlayer();
  createHUD();
}

private void createHUD() {
  HUD hud = new HUD();

  scoreText = new Text(16, 784, res.font, "0123456789", new
    TextOptions(HorizontalAlign.LEFT), vbom);
  scoreText.setAnchorCenter(0, 1);
  hud.attachChild(scoreText);

  camera.setHUD(hud);
}
```

This is all that is needed to attach the text to the HUD. We added a new method called `createHUD()` for convenience. In this method, we created a new `hud` object and attached the text to it. Finally, we passed our `hud` object to our camera.

If you want to destroy the HUD, simply call the following function:

```
camera.setHUD(null);
```

It's important to remember that the HUD is a property of the camera. When we switch to another scene, we have to remove the HUD.

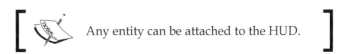 Any entity can be attached to the HUD.

Working with toasts

Another way to output text on the screen is using **toasts**. A toast is a simple message widget that can provide feedback about an operation in progress. It's a core Android widget, not an AndEngine component, but we can nevertheless use it in our game.

The easiest way to show a toast is to use a static method provided by the `Toast` class. In a general Android app, we can simply call this as follows:

```
Toast.makeText(activity, "Hello World", Toast.LENGTH_LONG).show();
```

We can also call a toast inside the activity itself. This can be done as follows:

```
Toast.makeText(this, "Hello World", Toast.LENGTH_LONG).show();
```

The `makeText()` method creates the `Toast` object. It takes three parameters: the context (activity), the text to show, and the length of the toast, which can be one of the following two types:

- `Toast.LENGTH_LONG`
- `Toast.LENGTH_SHORT`

Finally, we call the `show()` method on the newly created `Toast` object.

However, if we try to call this object inside the game, it won't work. This is because the `Toast` object must be created and dispatched in the UI thread. This thread is also called the main thread. AndEngine uses this thread to set up the engine and, as with every other Android application, to dispatch events from the UI to the components. This is the reason why it is called both the main and the UI thread.

Most of the actions in the game are happening in the update thread. So, when we want to use an Android widget such as a toast, we must tell the system to run the code in the UI thread. Every activity has a method called `runOnUiThread()`. Let's make use of it. Change the `populate()` method in the `GameScene` class as follows:

```
@Override
public void populate() {
  createBackground();
  createPlayer();
  createHUD();

  activity.runOnUiThread(new Runnable() {
    @Override
    public void run() {
      Toast.makeText(activity, "Hello world!",
        Toast.LENGTH_LONG).show();
    }
  });
}
```

The `runOnUiThread()` method expects an instance of a class implementing the `Runnable` interface, which must implement a `run()` method. We are creating an anonymous inner class implementing the method. An anonymous class is a locally instantiated class without a name. It's a Java statement that can be used anywhere where we can use a regular class. It's instantiated the same way, using the operator new; in this case, it's a class of type `Runnable`. It can be a child of a class or an implementation of an interface. It's useful when the class is used only once.

When we run the code now, there will be a small message saying **Hello world!** for a few seconds and then it will disappear on its own.

Localization

When we speak about application or game **localization** (or L10N, which means L followed by 10 letters and N), we generally mean supporting multiple languages. Another term is **internationalization** (or I18N), which means adapting the game to different regions. An example of I18N would be supporting both metric and imperial systems of units or supporting multiple date formats.

Localization in Android is very simple. The first step is to keep all the strings separate from the code. Instead of hardcoding Hello world!, we put this string into an XML resource file called strings.xml. This file is located at res/values/.

 Keeping the strings separated from the code is a good practice even when we support only one language.

When we created the application, the Eclipse new app wizard already put some strings there. The following code shows how the file should look:

```xml
<?xml version="1.0" encoding="utf-8"?>
<resources>

    <string name="app_name">LearningAndEngine</string>
    <string name="action_settings">Settings</string>
    <string name="hello_world">Hello world!</string>

</resources>
```

Each string has a name that we use to identify it in the code. It's important to use a self-explanatory name. The value is then the real string that will be printed to the screen. Instead of a hardcoded string, we then use the following:

```java
Toast.makeText(activity, activity.getString(R.string.hello_world),
    Toast.LENGTH_LONG).show();
```

The getString() method is used to retrieve the string based on an integer constant. These constants are located in a generated class simply called R. This class is generated automatically based on the XML file.

To use our strings, we must import the correct R class as follows:
```
import is.kul.learningandengine.R;
```
There is also a default class called android.R, which contains some commonly used strings such as R.string.yes and R.string.no.

To add another language, simply create a folder named res/values-code, where code is the language code, for example, de for German, es for Spanish, or cs for Czech. Then, copy the strings.xml file to the folder and translate the values to the desired language.

The file in the values directory serves as a default fallback option. The other language files don't have to contain all values from the default file. Let's say the application is running on a Spanish language phone, and we have only translated the hello_world string. Android will automatically use the language file based on the settings of the phone. But, when the application requests the app_name string, the value is not found in the Spanish language file and the value from the default file will be returned. If the application is running on a device with language settings that are not supported by the game at all, the default values will be used too.

The default file must always contain all values. In cases where there are more values in the specific language file and the app requests one of those extra strings on a device with different language settings, the app will crash.

The following screenshot shows the directory structure, and the new language file looks for the Czech language:

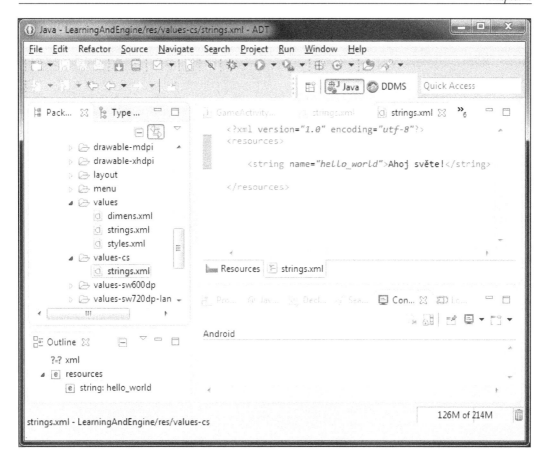

 The localization is not limited to the strings. The same principle works for any resource directory. This can be used to change the layout for different regions or to change image files based on language settings.

Debug output

The last option that we will learn about is using Android's debug output to LogCat. LogCat is an Android logger that can be accessed through the adb tool, and it is available in Eclipse as well. Logging, in general, is a way to output text that a developer needs to see but should stay hidden from the user.

To open the LogCat tab, go to **Window** | **Show View** | **Others...** and search for LogCat.

If an Android device is already connected, LogCat will immediately show some log messages. The following screenshot shows an example of what a LogCat output looks like:

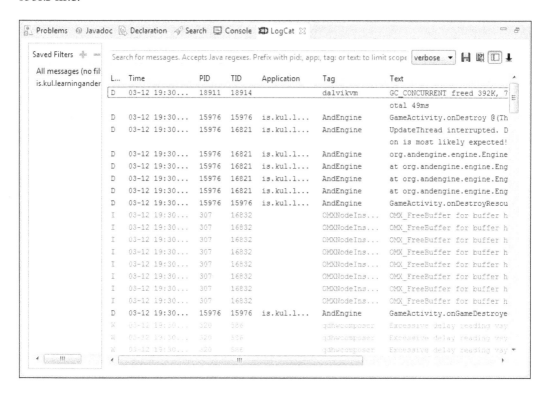

The log messages have the following attributes:

- **Log Level**: This is the severity of the message. It can be verbose, debug, info, warning, error, or assert (also known as **what a terrible failure** (**WTF**)). It is indicated by one letter only.

- **Time**: This is the timestamp when the message was added.

- **PID**: This is the process ID of the app that printed the message.

- **TID**: This is the thread ID.

- **Application**: This is identified by the package name.

- **Tag**: This is the custom identifier.

- **Text**: This is the custom message.

We can filter the messages by level and also use filtering to show only messages containing a certain string or tag.

Logging to LogCat from AndEngine

To call the logger in the code, we can use the Android Log class or the AndEngine Debug class. The following code snippets show a few examples to use logging:

```
Log.v("AndEngine", "This is a very detailed message");
Debug.v("This is a very detailed message");

Log.i("AndEngine", "Info level message");
Debug.i("AndEngine", "Info level message");

try {
  doSomethingDangerous();
} catch (Exception e) {
  Log.e("AndEngine", "Oops!", e);
  Debug.e("Oops!", e);
}

Debug.setDebugLevel(DebugLevel.ERROR);
Log.i("AndEngine", "This message still will be printed");
Debug.i("AndEngine", "This will not be printed, current level is
  ERROR");

Log.wtf("AndEngine", "This should never happen");
```

The first example is a verbose message using the Android Log class. The second example is the same as the first, just using the AndEngine Debug class. Notice that the tag is missing. The default tag AndEngine will be used.

The third and fourth examples show that both classes can be used in the same way. The try and catch blocks use logging with an extra parameter. In these two cases, the exception will be printed in LogCat with a full stack trace.

AndEngine has a method to set the debug level, which means messages below that level won't be printed. The levels are sorted by severity.

Finally, there is an example of the wtf log level, which is not implemented in AndEngine. It is usually used as a marker that the program entered a branch that should never have been reached. For example, when we expect the program to exit at a certain point, we can put the wft() message after the exit command. If the message gets printed, we will know that the exit was not successful.

Logging best practices

All exceptions should be logged and empty `catch` blocks avoided. Even if the exception is expected to happen sometimes, we should always at least print it to the log using the warning level, because the exception could happen for a different reason than the expected one.

The following is an explanation of what each of the levels mean:

- **Verbose**: This is used for low-level debugging, such as the position of the main character.
- **Debug**: These are messages that could be useful to determine where something went wrong. For example, a message at the end of a method to determine whether the method successfully finished.
- **Info**: This is used for important events, such as when the engine is successfully created.
- **Warning**: This is used when something is not quite right but it's not a bug. As an example, let's imagine we want to submit the high score to a server. If it fails, the game can continue, but the warning should be printed.
- **Error**: This is used for exceptions and errors that we will need to analyze and solve.
- **Assert**: This is the WTF level.

Log messages should also be optimized. Let's take the following simple logging message that prints the character's position to a log:

```
Log.d("AndEngine", "Position: " + x + ", " + y);
```

The Java compiler creates a `StringBuilder` object, uses three method calls, and then throws the `StringBuilder` object away. If this is done inside a game loop of a game that shows 60 frames per second, it can have a big impact on performance.

What we should do instead is one of the three following options. The first option is as follows:

```
if (BuildConfig.DEBUG) {
  Log.d("AndEngine", "Position: " + x + ", " + y);
}
```

`BuildConfig.DEBUG` is Android's built-in property that should be set automatically to `false` during the export of the production APK file. It is recommended to clean the project before trying to export it, because this constant is located in one of the generated classes. The second option is our own Boolean property, which we can add to the `GameActivity` class as follows:

```
if (GameActivity.DEBUG) {
  Debug.d("Position: " + x + ", " + y);
}
```

Finally, the third option is AndEngine's built-in mechanism to test for the current debug level. This is shown in the following code:

```
if (Debug.getDebugLevel().isSameOrLessThan(DebugLevel.DEBUG)) {
  Debug("Position: " + x + ", " + y);
}
```

When using any of these, the concatenation will not be called if the condition is `false`. When using AndEngine's `Debug` class, we can set the debug level to NONE to avoid printing anything.

Summary

In this chapter, we learned the basics of text output. Now, we are able to print text to the screen, keep it in view by attaching it to an HUD, and support multiple languages. We have discussed the caveats and limitations of AndEngine text implementation.

We also learned how to use Android logging to print development text and how to access it.

In the next chapter, we will look into touch and tilt controls and start moving our character around.

Basic Interactions

It's time to learn how to make the game interactive. In this chapter, we will first see how to create a basic animation that will allow us to move the character from one place to another. We will also learn the basics of collision detection.

Then, we will look into the different sensors that Android devices have, how to read them, and how to use those readings. More specifically, we are going to use the **touchscreen** and **accelerometer**, and we will use them to move the main character around the screen.

The second part of this chapter will cover the specifics of different threads used in AndEngine in detail. We will discuss the dangers of mixing threads and common mistakes made by beginners to AndEngine.

A simple animation

There are two ways of creating an animation. First, our sprite can give multiple frames and we animate the sprite by changing the frames in time. The second way is using tweens (short for in-between).

An animated sprite

The `AnimatedSprite` class is simply a tiled sprite with the added functionality to change tiles in time. Let's change the `GameScene` class temporarily to see how an animated sprite works. This is shown in the following code:

```
AnimatedSprite fly;

@Override
```

```
public void populate() {
  ...

  fly = new AnimatedSprite(240, 200, res.enemyTextureRegion
    , vbom);
  fly.animate(125);
  attachChild(fly);
}
```

The first line creates the animated sprite. It works exactly the same way as any other sprite. We simply specify the location on the screen, the tiled texture region, and the Vertex Buffer Object manager.

The `animate()` method starts the animation. It takes a single parameter or multiple parameters. The simplest way is to pass one float value that specifies for how long in milliseconds each frame is displayed. However, sometimes we want to specify different times, or show only some of the frames, and so on. The following are some examples of the `animate()` method:

- `fly.animate(new long[]{100, 200}, new int[]{1, 0}, false);`: The first parameter is an array of durations and the second parameter is the frames to be displayed. The third parameter means we don't want the animation looped. In this case, the call will play the second frame (numbered as 1) first for 100 milliseconds and then the first frame (numbered as 0) for 200 milliseconds. Then, it will stop there.

- `aSprite.animate(new long[]{100, 200, 150}, 7, 9, true);`: This call is similar to the first one, but instead of specifying the frames one by one, we only specify the start (7) and end (9) frames. However, we must specify times for each of them.

- `aSprite.animate(animationData)`: This is a more advanced way to call the `animate()` method. Here, `animationData` is an implementation of the `AnimatedSprite.IAnimationData` interface. This is a bit advanced, but when we need some really complicated animation that is not covered by the existing methods, it might help us.

Finally, we attach the sprite to the scene. After running the application, we should see a fly below our character. The fly should be flapping its wings. This is shown in the following screenshot:

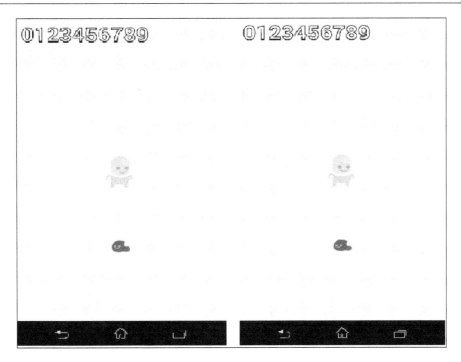

Entity modifiers

AndEngine offers a very simple way of creating tweens using **entity modifiers**. Tweens are simple math equations that allow us to change a property value to another value continuously. Basic examples of such tweens are movement, rotation, scaling, and color change. Entity modifiers allow us to do exactly that.

The great thing about entity modifiers is that they can be applied to any entity, and they can be chained or run in parallel. It's also possible to have an entity modifier listener that will be called when the modifier starts and finishes. As mentioned before, an entity modifier is a tween. The basic math equation to transform one value to another is a simple linear equation. But, there are more equations called ease functions that allow us to create interesting effects.

The following are a few examples:

```
fly.registerEntityModifier(new RotationModifier(2, 0, 360));
```

The preceding code will make the fly rotate once from 0 degrees to 360 degrees (one full turn). Now, consider the following code:

```
fly.registerEntityModifier(new LoopEntityModifier(new
  RotationModifier(2, 0, 360)));
```

By adding looping, the fly will rotate indefinitely. Lastly, consider the following code:

```
fly.registerEntityModifier(new LoopEntityModifier(new
  RotationModifier(2, 0, 360, EaseExponentialIn.getInstance())));
```

In this case, the fly will rotate slowly at the beginning and then faster near the end. This is the same as the exponential function used.

> See the hierarchy of the IEntityModifier interface in Eclipse to see all available modifiers. To do this, simply open the interface, click on the name, and press *F4*. We can see the modifiers in action in the AndEngineExamples project that is available in the GitHub repository. It is also available on the Google Play store under the same name as a working application.

In the next part, we are going to see examples of the move modifiers.

User input

AndEngine uses a simple abstraction layer above the Android user input handlers. We are going to use the touchscreen and the accelerometer, but it is of course possible to use any other sensors that are not implemented in AndEngine by directly calling the Android SDK methods.

Touchscreen

Let's start with the touchscreen, because it's the most common way of getting user input in smartphones and tablets. The Android system is handling the touchscreen itself and it is firing touch events. These touch events are caught and processed by AndEngine. We are going to handle them using **event listeners**.

Touch events

Touch events in AndEngine handle five basic motion events from the Android SDK. In this case, the terms motion and touch event can be used interchangeably. These five events are as follows:

- ACTION_DOWN: This is the most basic event; it happens at the beginning of a touch.

- ACTION_MOVE: When the touch starts and the user drags their finger or pen on the screen, move events are triggered.

- ACTION_OUTSIDE: This happens when the motion event leaves the current view. This can happen, for example, when a warning dialog pops up during the move event.

- ACTION_CANCEL: This happens when the user touches the screen inside AndEngine's view and drags it outside its boundaries. We are not going to see this, because we will only use the full-screen view. This should be treated as the ACTION_UP event, but with no reaction performed.

- ACTION_UP: This happens at the end of the touch.

> It is important to always check what event just happened. Each physical touch usually generates at least the down and up events and sometimes down, move, and up. Usually, we only want to perform an action in one of the events.

There are two basic ways to handle events in AndEngine. First, each scene has its own touch listener. Second, every entity that has an area can override the onAreaTouched() method.

The scene touch listener

Global events that don't belong to any specific entity can be handled in the scene touch listener. A good example is the go-to on touch functionality. The user touches the screen and the character will move to that place. Each listener can return a Boolean value, irrespective of whether the event was handled or not. If not, a child scene or specific entities will be called to handle the event. If yes, the event is marked as handled and the handling stops here.

Let's change our GameScene code to handle scene touch events and move our character. Again, edit the populate() method and add the following lines:

```
@Override
public void populate() {
  ...

  setOnSceneTouchListener(new IOnSceneTouchListener() {

    @Override
    public boolean onSceneTouchEvent(Scene pScene, TouchEvent
      pSceneTouchEvent) {
      if (pSceneTouchEvent.isActionDown()) {
        player.clearEntityModifiers();
```

```
        player.registerEntityModifier(new MoveModifier(1,
          player.getX(), player.getY(), pSceneTouchEvent.getX(),
          pSceneTouchEvent.getY()));
        return true;
      }
      return false;
    }
  });
}
```

The setOnSceneTouchListener() method overrides any listener that is currently set. Only one listener per scene is allowed. Here, we are creating an anonymous class that implements the IOnSceneTouchListener interface, which has only one method: onSceneTouchEvent().

In this method, we first check whether the touch event is down. Next, we will clear all entity modifiers. If we do not do this, each touch would add one modifier that would try to move the character to a new location. The character would move chaotically. The clearEntityModifiers() method removes all the modifiers. In the case of a move modifier, the character will stop at the current position.

Finally, we return a true value, which means we completely handled the touch event. In the case any other event was triggered, we return a false value, which means the other events are handled elsewhere.

In our case, it doesn't matter whether we return a true or false value. But in a more complex scenario, such as overlapping entities, we might want to return a true value to indicate that only the first (topmost) entity will register the touch.

The entity touch area

Any entity can handle its own touches. The simplest example of such usage is a button. Instead of catching the event in the screen touch listener and then looking for the entity that was touched, we simply add a listener to the entity and let it handle the touch itself.

Each entity implements the ITouchArea interface. For this to work properly, the entity must properly define its area. This topic is a bit advanced, but for now, it's enough to know that all the basic entities such as primitive shapes and sprites correctly define the touchable area by default and we do not have to implement it ourselves.

Let's update our `Player` class code. We simply override the `onAreaTouched()`
method. By default, this method only returns a `false` value, which means that
it doesn't handle the events. Consider the following code:

```
@Override
public boolean onAreaTouched(TouchEvent pSceneTouchEvent,
  float pTouchAreaLocalX, float pTouchAreaLocalY) {
  if (pSceneTouchEvent.isActionDown()) {
    clearEntityModifiers();
    return true;
  } else if (pSceneTouchEvent.isActionMove()) {
    setPosition(pSceneTouchEvent.getX(), pSceneTouchEvent.
      getY());
    return true;
  }
  return false;
}
```

We are handling two events here. Firstly, in the case of the down touch event, we
clear the modifiers and return a `true` value. If we do not clear the modifiers, there
might be a movement modifier from the scene touch in place. If we do not return a
`true` value, the chain of handlers would continue and the scene would handle the
event. Secondly, on the move event, we update the position of the sprite.

Optionally, we could handle the up event as well, but the move
should end at the same place as where the up event happens.

Lastly, we need to register the touch area in the scene. Otherwise, the
`onAreaTouched()` method will never be triggered. We register the area in the
`GameScene` class, in the `populate()` method. This is shown in the following code:

```
@Override
public void populate() {

  ...

  registerTouchArea(player);
}
```

With this code in place, together with the scene touch listener, the main character
will move either when we tap on the destination or when we tap on the character
itself and drag it around.

Touch area bindings

Sometimes, we touch an entity, which triggers the down event, but then we move our finger away and end the touch outside the entity. In that case, the up event is not registered for the entity. A similar thing can happen when dragging an entity and our finger leaves the entity area. For example, it happens when the drag is slower than the actual physical motion.

In such cases, we can use the `setTouchAreaBindingOnActionDownEnabled()` and `setTouchAreaBindingOnActionMoveEnabled()` methods. When set to `true`, a binding is created between an event and an entity, and even after our finger leaves the entity, the entity will still receive notifications, such as an `ACTION_UP` event, from the motion in progress.

Accelerometer

There are many sensors available in the Android SDK, but not all need to be implemented. This is the case for a thermometer, for example. Fortunately, an accelerometer is available in most devices.

Using the accelerometer in AndEngine is simple. The engine offers a listener interface, `IAccelerationListener`, that has two methods, `onAccelerationAccuracyChanged` and `onAccelerationChanged`. We will be using the second method.

 The first method is rarely called in the case of an accelerometer and we can ignore it. However, in the case of other sensors, such as GPS accuracy, it can be crucial. It is called when the accuracy of readings is changed. For example, when the phone enters a building, the GPS signal becomes weak and this method will be called. An accelerometer doesn't suffer from such problems, but theoretically, the method can be called.

Let's start with creating the acceleration listener. The easiest way is to let our `GameScene` class implement the interface itself and implement both the methods. Consider the following code:

```
public class GameScene extends AbstractScene implements
IAccelerationListener {

  @Override
  public void onAccelerationAccuracyChanged(AccelerationData
    pAccelerationData) {
```

```
    }

    @Override  public void onAccelerationChanged(AccelerationData
      pAccelerationData) {
    }
  }
```

We will ignore the first method and leave it empty. The second method is being called whenever the acceleration changes. In Android, there are several delay settings for the accelerometer. For games, the lowest setting is used and AndEngine uses it by default, which means the accelerometer is updated very often.

 Don't worry about optimizing this right now. It is dangerous to put any heavy calculations in this method, so optimize only when you see a problem.

Each time the method is called, the AccelerationData object will be filled with values from the current reading of the accelerometer. It is possible to get the device orientation, the accelerometer accuracy, and most importantly, the three accelerometer values for all the three axes.

To make our character move according to the tilt of the device, we implement the onAccelerationChanged method in the following way:

```
    float lastX = 0;
    @Override
    public void onAccelerationChanged(final AccelerationData
      pAccelerationData) {
      if (Math.abs(pAccelerationData.getX() - lastX) > 0.5) {
        if (pAccelerationData.getX() > 0) {
          player.turnRight();
        } else {
          player.turnLeft();
        }
        lastX = pAccelerationData.getX();
      }

      player.setX(player.getX() + pAccelerationData.getX());
    }
```

We are doing two things here. First, we are making the character face the direction of the movement. It looks a bit complicated. We are saving the previous x value of the accelerometer and changing the facing direction only when the difference reaches a certain threshold. This is to prevent twitching when the accelerometer value is very close to zero.

Try changing the value 0.5 to something smaller or even a negative value (then the condition is always true). You will notice twitching.

The last line makes the character move on the *x* axis based on the tilt of the device.

Finally, we must enable the accelerometer and register the listener in the engine. Simply add the following line of code to the `populate()` method:

```
@Override
public void populate() {
    ...
    engine.enableAccelerationSensor(activity, this);
}
```

We must register the listener only after we have created the player. Otherwise, the accelerometer could get a reading before we have initialized the `Player` object, which would cause a null pointer exception.

The `enableAccelerationSensor` method takes two parameters. The first one is our main activity and the second one is the accelerometer listener, which is our scene; therefore, we pass it.

Pausing and resuming the accelerometer

When the game is paused, we might want to pause the accelerometer for two reasons. First, if the accelerometer is used as an input, we don't want any input when the game is paused. The other reason is battery usage. The accelerometer drains the battery; therefore, it is beneficial to disable it when it is not needed and then enable it again on resuming. We can use our `onPause()` and `onResume()` methods in the `GameScene` class as follows:

```
@Override
public void onPause() {
    engine.disableAccelerationSensor(activity);
}

@Override
public void onResume() {
    engine.enableAccelerationSensor(activity, this);
}
```

Collision detection

One of the most basic interactions in games is a collision of two entities. There are several ways to detect collisions. In this chapter, we will cover basic entity collisions. The other popular methods are pixel-perfect collisions and physics engine collisions.

We are going to look at physics engine collisions in *Chapter 6, Physics*. There is an extension for pixel-perfect collisions as well, but it is unofficial and created for an older version of AndEngine.

The basic collision detection works with the underlying geometry. For example, a sprite is actually a texture drawn on a quad (two triangles). When creating sprites that will be a part of collision detection, we should take extra care about their bounding boxes.

Let's see a bad example of a bounding box. The following figure shows a texture that will be used to create a sprite:

The following figure shows how it will look when detecting collisions. The black bounding box is a boundary of the underlying geometries. The red area is the actual collision.

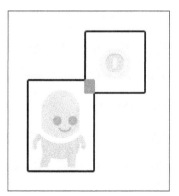

We can define a polygonal textured mesh to make the collision detection more precise. However, that is a very advanced technique, and for our purposes, the rectangle bounding boxes will suffice. We only need to create them as small as possible.

Handling collisions

There are two possible ways of using basic collision detection. A collision handler is useful when trying to detect the collision once. Detecting collisions in the onManagedUpdate method is better when there is a need to continuously determine whether two objects are colliding.

Collision handlers

A collision handler implementation in AndEngine is in a class simply called CollisionHandler. This class implements the IUpdateHandler interface. Update handlers are special classes that can be registered in the engine and they are called in each update cycle of the engine.

To add a collision handler that will detect a collision between the player character and the fly, we simply add the following code to the populate() method in the GameScene class:

```
@Override
public void populate() {
  ...

  ICollisionCallback myCollisionCallback = new ICollisionCallback
    () {

    @Override
    public boolean onCollision(IShape pCheckShape, IShape
      pTargetShape) {
      fly.setColor(Color.RED);
      return false;
    }
  };

  CollisionHandler myCollisionHandler = new
    CollisionHandler(myCollisionCallback, fly, player);
  registerUpdateHandler(myCollisionHandler);
}
```

The first thing we do is create a collision callback. The callback method onCollision() will be called automatically when the collision handler detects a collision. What we do is change the fly's color to red.

Only the light parts of the fly will change color. The `setColor()` method works like a color filter. If something is black, it will stay black with any filter.

The callback returns a `false` value if no more collision detection is needed or a `true` value to indicate that the rest of the collisions should be handled too.

Next, we create the handler and pass both `player` and `fly` to it. The collision handler can also accept a list of entities, and in that case, it will check each entity against all the others.

Finally, we register the collision handler as an update handler. When the player sprite collides with the fly, the fly will change color. The color change is permanent.

The collidesWith method

The `collidesWith` method belongs to each entity and can be used anywhere. It is simple and returns a `true` value if the current entity is colliding with another entity. We are going to use it in the `onManagedUpdate()` method to perform continuous collision detection. The method is called for every entity attached to the scene in each cycle of the game loop.

We can override the `onManagedUpdate()` method when creating the entity. For example, we use our `fly` object and add the collision detection there. To do this, let's follow these steps:

1. Change the initialization of the `fly` object to the following:

    ```
    fly = new AnimatedSprite(240, 200, res.enemyTextureRegion,
      vbom) {

      @Override
      protected void onManagedUpdate(float pSecondsElapsed) {
        super.onManagedUpdate(pSecondsElapsed);
        if (collidesWith(player)) {
          setScale(2);
        } else {
          setScale(1);
        }
      }
    };
    ```

    We call the parent classes on the `onManagedUpdate()` method first, because there might be some important calculations done.

2. Then, we check for the collision, and if it is true, we set the scale to double. In this case, the fly will be enlarged when it collides with the player character, and it will return to normal size when they stop colliding.

3. With both collision detections in place, we can run the application. There should be no change at first. Have a look at the following screenshot:

4. When the character moves close to the fly, both collision detectors get triggered. The fly will turn red and expand. The collision is not perfect, which is clearly visible in the following screenshot. The bounding boxes already overlap, but the actual characters don't.

5. Finally, when the character moves away, the fly will stay red and shrink back to normal size. This is shown in the following screenshot:

Using correct threads to perform actions

As already mentioned in *Chapter 4*, *HUD and Text Display*, AndEngine uses different threads for different actions. This makes sense, because the thread that takes care of drawing entities should not be affected by the thread that registers touches.

The two basic threads are the UI (sometimes called main) and update threads. There are certain actions that must be performed in the correct thread. Actions such as showing a toast, dialog, or any other Android view manipulation must be done in the UI thread. Other actions such as manipulating entities must be done in the update thread.

The most common problem with AndEngine is a crash after detaching an entity when a modifier is finished or detaching an entity after performing a touch. There exist a lot of misconceptions among the people in the AndEngine community about this. You will often hear that the problem is caused by detaching the entity in the wrong thread.

However, that is not true because AndEngine takes care of the threads and runs even the touch events, listeners, and update handlers in the update thread. To keep alive the misconception, using the `runOnUpdateThread()` method actually helps.

Let's see an example of the problem. The basic use case here is to remove the player character as soon as it stops moving after a scene touch. The following code snippet is the relevant part of the `populate()` method in the `GameScene` class:

```
setOnSceneTouchListener(new IOnSceneTouchListener() {

  @Override
  public boolean onSceneTouchEvent(Scene pScene, TouchEvent
    pSceneTouchEvent) {
    if (pSceneTouchEvent.isActionDown()) {
      Debug.i("Touching scene in Thread: " +
        Thread.currentThread().getName());
      IEntityModifierListener myEntityModifierListener = new
        IEntityModifierListener() {

        @Override
        public void onModifierStarted(IModifier<IEntity>
          pModifier, IEntity pItem) {
        }

        @Override
        public void onModifierFinished(IModifier<IEntity>
          pModifier, IEntity pItem) {
```

```
            Debug.i("Detaching player in Thread: " +
                Thread.currentThread().getName());
            player.detachSelf();
          }
        };

      player.clearEntityModifiers();
      player.registerEntityModifier(new MoveModifier(1,
        player.getX(), player.getY(),
        pSceneTouchEvent.getX(), pSceneTouchEvent.getY(),
        myEntityModifierListener));
      return true;
    }
    return false;
    }
  });
```

We have added log messages that will print the name of the current thread into
LogCat. There are two possible options. The UI thread is identified as the main
thread and the update thread is identified as **UpdateThread**.

Next, we create the `myEntityModifierListener` class that will listen to the modifier
events, and when the modifier finishes, it will try to detach the player sprite from
the scene. But, when we run the game now and tap the screen, the player sprite
will move there and then the game will crash with an `ArrayIndexOutOfBounds`
exception. Now, the common answer to the question why would be that we are not
detaching the player in the update thread. But, the log says otherwise, as shown in
the following screenshot:

```
I  07-25 11:23:28.600   29676  29705  is.kul.1...   AndEngine     Touching scene in Thread: UpdateThread
I  07-25 11:23:29.561   29676  29705  is.kul.1...   AndEngine     Detaching player in Thread: UpdateThread
```

What is actually happening is that AndEngine is going through all N entities and
performing all the required actions. At one point, it is handling the player entity,
and it registers that the modifier has finished and calls the method of the modifier
listener. There, we try to detach it. This still works but the engine will remove the
entity from the list of handled entities, because it's detached and therefore no
longer needs handling.

Then, the control is returned to the current iteration of the list of entities. The list
has changed in the meantime; it now contains N-1 entities. But the engine still
iterates as if there are N entities and this causes the exception when trying to
fetch the last element, which is no longer there.

The following code shows a typical example of how to fix this problem. We will add a `runOnUpdateThread()` method call that will cause the code to execute at a different time.

```
setOnSceneTouchListener(new IOnSceneTouchListener() {

  @Override
  public boolean onSceneTouchEvent(Scene pScene, TouchEvent
    pSceneTouchEvent) {
    if (pSceneTouchEvent.isActionDown()) {

      IEntityModifierListener myEntityModifierListener = new
        IEntityModifierListener() {

        @Override
        public void onModifierStarted(IModifier<IEntity>
          pModifier, IEntity pItem) {
        }

        @Override
        public void onModifierFinished(IModifier<IEntity>
          pModifier, IEntity pItem) {

          res.activity.runOnUpdateThread(new Runnable() {
            @Override
            public void run() {
              player.detachSelf();
            }
          });

        }
      };

      player.clearEntityModifiers();
      player.registerEntityModifier(new MoveModifier(1,
        player.getX(), player.getY(),
        pSceneTouchEvent.getX(), pSceneTouchEvent.getY(),
        myEntityModifierListener));
      return true;
    }
    return false;
  }
});
```

We have added the `runOnUpdateThread()` method call and it fixes the problem. It might lead us to the assumption that we were using the wrong thread, but in fact this call simply delays the action to the beginning of the next game loop iteration, and therefore, will detach the player before the processing of all the entities starts. But it will happen in the update thread nevertheless.

Summary

In this chapter, we have learned the basics of user input. We have covered the touchscreen and accelerometer and seen how to make the game respond to touch and tilt events using animations and how to deal with collisions. Lastly, we have looked into the most common mistake that happens when working with entities and threads and how to deal with those problems.

In the next chapter, we are going to add physics to our game. We will learn about different physics bodies, forces, and how to detect collisions using the physics engine.

6
Physics

In the last chapter, we introduced one of the ways to move a character in AndEngine using the entity modifiers. However, for our game, we are going to use a physics engine. In this chapter, we will first introduce the physics engine used in AndEngine. We are also going to explain basic physics terms, such as force and velocity, and how they are used in AndEngine. We will cover the limitations of the physics engine too.

In the second part of this chapter, we will implement some of the actions of our character using the physics engine and accelerometer readings. We will also add platforms and the enemy to the game and define them as physics **bodies**.

The physics engine

AndEngine uses the Android port of the Box2D physics engine. Box2D is very popular in games, including the most popular ones such as *Angry Birds*, and many game engines and frameworks use Box2D to simulate physics. It is free, open source, and written in C++, and it is available on multiple platforms. AndEngine offers a Java wrapper API for the C++ Box2D backend, and therefore, no prior C++ knowledge is required to use it.

Box2D can simulate 2D **rigid** bodies. A rigid body is a simplification of a solid body with no deformations. Such objects do not exist in reality, but if we limit the bodies to those moving much slower than the speed of light, we can say that solid bodies are also rigid.

Box2D uses real-world units and works with physics terms. A position in a scene in AndEngine is defined in pixel coordinates, whereas in Box2D, it is defined in meters. AndEngine uses a pixel to meter conversion ratio. The default value is 32 pixels per meter.

Basic terms

Box2D works with something we call a **physics world**. There are bodies and forces in the physics world. Every body in the simulation has the following few basic properties:

- Position
- Orientation
- Mass (in kilograms)
- Velocity (in meters per second)
- Torque (or angular velocity in radians per second)

Forces are applied to bodies and the following Newton's laws of motion apply:

- The first law, *An object that is not moving or moving with constant velocity will stay that way until a force is applied to it*, can be tweaked a bit
- The second law, *Force is equal to mass multiplied by acceleration*, is especially important to understand what will happen when we apply force to different objects
- The third law, *For every action, there is an equal and opposite reaction*, is a bit flexible when using different types of bodies

Body types

There are three different body types in Box2D, and each one is used for a different purpose. The body types are as follows:

- **Static body**: This doesn't have velocity and forces do not apply to a static body. If another body collides with a static body, it will not move. Static bodies do not collide with other static and kinematic bodies. Static bodies usually represent walls, floors, and other immobile things. In our case, they will represent platforms which don't move.
- **Kinematic body**: This has velocity, but forces don't apply to it. If a kinematic body is moving and a dynamic body collides with it, the kinematic body will continue in its original direction. Kinematic bodies also do not collide with other static and kinematic bodies. Kinematic bodies are useful to create moving platforms, which is exactly how we are going to use them.

- **Dynamic body**: A dynamic body has velocity and forces apply to it. Dynamic bodies are the closest to real-world bodies and they collide with all types of bodies. We are going to use a dynamic body for our main character.

 It is important to understand the consequences of choosing each body type. When we define gravity in Box2D, it will pull all dynamic bodies to the direction of the gravitational acceleration, but static bodies will remain still and kinematic bodies will either remain still or keep moving in their set direction as if there was no gravity.

Fixtures

Every body is composed of one or more **fixtures**. Each fixture has the following four basic properties:

- **Shape**: In Box2D, fixtures can be circles, rectangles, and polygons
- **Density**: This determines the mass of the fixture
- **Friction**: This plays a major role in body interactions
- **Elasticity**: This is sometimes called restitution and determines how bouncy the object is

There are also special properties of fixtures such as filters and filter categories, which we will cover in *Chapter 8, Advanced Physics*, and a single Boolean property called **sensor**.

Shapes

The position of fixtures and their shapes in the body determine the overall shape, mass, and the center of gravity of the body.

The upcoming figure is an example of a body that consists of three fixtures. The fixtures do not need to connect. They are part of one body, and that means their positions relative to each other will not change.

The red dot represents the body's center of gravity. The green rectangle is a static body and the other three shapes are part of a dynamic body. Gravity pulls the whole body down, but the square will not fall.

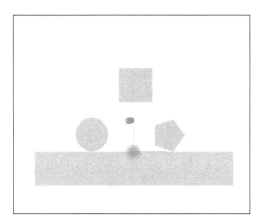

Density

Density determines how heavy the fixtures are. Because Box2D is a two-dimensional engine, we can imagine all objects to be one meter deep. In fact, it doesn't matter as long as we are consistent.

There are two bodies, each with a single circle fixture, in the following figure. The left circle is exactly twice as big as the right one, but the right one has double the density of the first one. The triangle is a static body and the rectangle and the circles are dynamic, creating a simple scale. When the simulation is run, the scales are balanced.

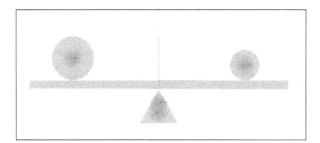

Friction

Friction defines how slippery a surface is. A body can consist of multiple fixtures with different friction values. When two bodies collide, the final friction is calculated from the point of collision based on the colliding fixtures.

Friction can be given a value between 0 and 1, where 0 means completely frictionless and 1 means super strong friction. Let's say we have a slope which is made of a body with a single fixture that has a friction value of 0.5, as shown in the following figure:

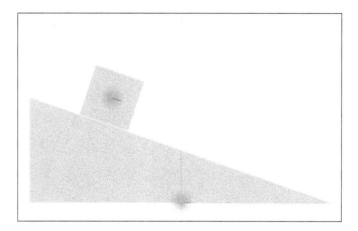

The other body consists of a single square fixture. If its friction is 0, the body slides very fast all the way down. If the friction is more than 0, then it would still slide, but slow down gradually. If the value is more than 0.25, it would still slide but not reach the end. Finally, with friction close to 1, the body will not move at all.

Elasticity

The coefficient of restitution is a ratio between the speeds before and after a collision, and for simplicity, we can call the material property elasticity. In the following figure, there are three circles and a rectangle representing a floor with restitution 0, which means not bouncy at all. The circles have restitutions (from left to right) of 1, 0.5, and 0.

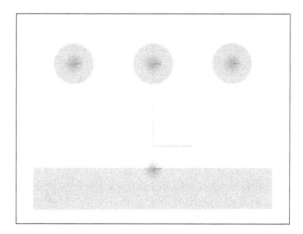

When this simulation is started, the three balls will fall with the same speed and touch the floor at the same time. However, after the first bounce, the first one will move upwards and climb all the way to the initial position. The middle one will bounce a little and keep bouncing less and less until it stops. The right one will not bounce at all. The following figure shows the situation after the first bounce:

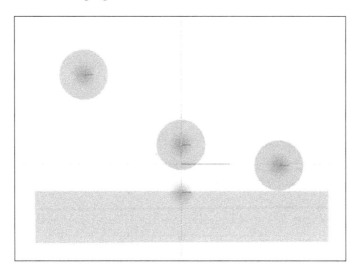

Sensor

When we need a fixture that detects collisions but is otherwise not affected by them and doesn't affect other fixtures and bodies, we use a sensor. A goal line in a 2D air hockey top-down game is a good example of a sensor. We want it to detect the disc passing through, but we don't want it to prevent the disc from entering the goal.

The physics world

The physics world is the whole simulation including all bodies with their fixtures, gravity, and other settings that influence the performance and quality of the simulation.

 Tweaking the physics world settings is important for large simulations with many objects. These settings include the number of steps performed per second and the number of velocity and position interactions per step.

The most important setting is gravity, which is determined by a vector of gravitational acceleration. Gravity in Box2D is simplified, but for the purpose of games, it is usually enough. Box2D works best when simulating a relatively small scene where objects are a few tens of meters big at most.

To simulate, for example, a planet's (radial) gravity, we would have to implement our own gravitational force and turn the Box2D built-in gravity off.

Forces and impulses

Both forces and impulses are used to make a body move. Gravity is nothing else but a constant application of a force. While it is possible to set the position and velocity of a body in Box2D directly, it is not the right way to do it, because it makes the simulation unrealistic.

To move a body properly, we need to apply a force or an impulse to it. These two things are almost the same. While forces are added to all the other forces and change the body velocity over time, impulses change the body velocity immediately. In fact, an impulse is defined as a force applied over time.

We can imagine a foam ball falling from the sky. When the wind starts blowing from the left, the ball will slowly change its trajectory. Impulse is more like a tennis racket that hits the ball in flight and changes its trajectory immediately.

There are two types of forces and impulses: linear and angular. Linear makes the body move left, right, up, and down, and angular makes the body spin around its center. Angular force is called **torque**.

Linear forces and impulses are applied at a given point, which will have different effects based on the position. The following figure shows a simple body with two fixtures and quite high friction, something like a carton box on a carpet. First, we apply force to the center of the large square fixture.

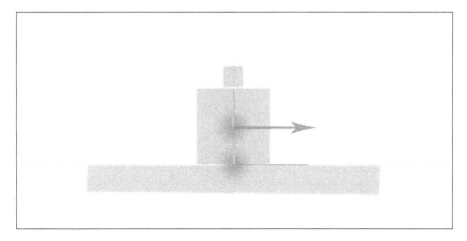

When the force is applied, the body simply moves on the ground to the right a little. This is shown in the following figure:

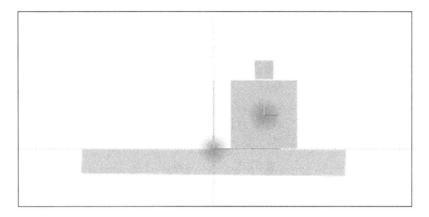

Second, we try to apply force to the upper-right corner of the large box. This is shown in the following figure:

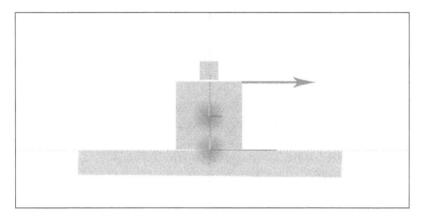

Using the same force at a different point, the body will be toppled to the right side. This is shown in the following figure:

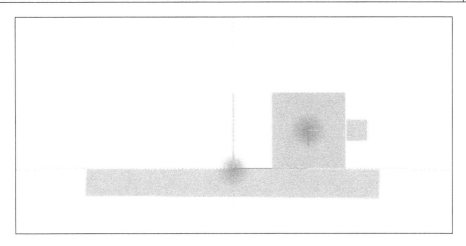

Joints

When a body is assembled from different fixtures, the fixtures never move relatively to each other. **Joints** link multiple bodies together. They can fix all degrees of freedom or fix only some of them. Joints are a more advanced topic that will be covered in *Chapter 8, Advanced Physics*.

Adding physics

We are going to add a physics world to our game and set it up with gravity. We will also make a physics body for the player character and add platforms. Finally, we will make the character move based on the tilt of our Android device. The physics extension should be already included in your game project since *Chapter 1, Setting Up an AndEngine Project*.

First, we must remove the code that we added in *Chapter 5, Basic Interactions*, when we were learning about modifiers, because we don't want the entity to be controlled by touch or drag-and-drop. We want it to be controlled by physics and gravity.

The following code snippet shows how the relevant parts of the cleaned up version of the GameScene class should look. The populate() method will be limited only to this code.

```
@Override
public void populate() {
  createBackground();
  createPlayer();
  createHUD();
  engine.enableAccelerationSensor(activity, this);
}
```

The onAccelerationChanged() method should look like the following code snippet:

```
float lastX = 0;
@Override
public void onAccelerationChanged(final AccelerationData
  pAccelerationData) {
  if (Math.abs(pAccelerationData.getX() - lastX) > 0.5) {
    if (pAccelerationData.getX() > 0) {
      player.turnRight();
    } else {
      player.turnLeft();
    }
    lastX = pAccelerationData.getX();
  }
}
```

We have removed the part that controls which direction the player is facing. We can also remove all unnecessary fields and imports now.

The final code of this chapter is available in the code bundle.

Adding a physics world

We start by adding a physics world to the game. It is very straightforward. Every Box2D port will have its equivalent of a physics world. The one in AndEngine is implemented as an update handler. The following code belongs to the GameScene class and adds and registers the physics world as an update handler:

```
private PhysicsWorld physicsWorld;

public GameScene() {
  super();
  physicsWorld = new PhysicsWorld(new Vector2(0, -
    SensorManager.GRAVITY_EARTH * 4), false);
```

```
    PlayerFactory.getInstance().create(vbom);
}

@Override
public void populate() {
  createBackground();
  createPlayer();
  createHUD();

  engine.enableAccelerationSensor(activity, this);
  registerUpdateHandler(physicsWorld);
}
```

When creating the physics world, two parameters are passed into the `physicsworld` class constructor. The first parameter is the gravity vector. We are using the value of Earth's gravity from the Android SDK multiplied by four to make the fall faster. The second parameter is a Boolean value that defines whether the engine should allow the sleeping of bodies. A body that comes to rest can be flagged as sleeping, which means it will no longer be simulated until something collides with it or a force is applied to it. This is a good optimization.

 Putting a physics body to sleep has its drawbacks too. If sleeping is turned on and the player character falls on a platform and stands still, it will enter the sleep state. When we change the gravitational vector afterwards, the player character will not be notified of this change and will remain in the sleep state.

Introducing a collidable entity

It's a good practice to encapsulate functionality of an entity within the entity itself. In simple tutorials, it's possible to add the body directly in the `GameScene` class. But we want to keep our code well organized.

We are going to deal with entities that will have a physics body and will be colliding with each other. Therefore, we are going to introduce an interface called `CollidableEntity` in the `is.kul.learningandengine.entity` package. This can be done as follows:

```
public interface CollidableEntity extends IEntity {
  public void setBody(Body body);
  public Body getBody();
  public String getType();
}
```

We want to have access to the physics body, and for the purpose of the collision, we want to know what kind of object it is.

Relation between physics bodies and entities

What we see in the game and how the actual physics bodies look can be two different things. Because the physics simulation can be very resource demanding, it's usually a good idea to simplify the bodies as much as possible. The following figure shows two examples of how bodies can relate to entities, and specifically to our case, sprites.

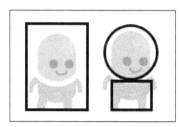

The first example is what we are going to use. The physics body is based on the sprite itself. There is some extra space that will cause the collisions to be triggered outside the actual player character, which might be noticeable in the game. For the collision between a platform and the feet, the box is sufficient. But for the collisions between the player character and the flying enemies, better approximation might be required. This is the easiest way to create a physics body.

The second option will produce better results when detecting collisions. We will get back to it in *Chapter 8*, *Advanced Physics*, when we are going to improve the physics simulation with some advanced techniques.

Adding a physics body to the player entity

The existing `Player` class will be our first colliding entity. Let's implement the `CollidableEntity` interface and add the required methods:

```
public class Player extends TiledSprite implements
  CollidableEntity {

...

  private Body body;
  public static final String TYPE = "Player";

...

  @Override
  public void setBody(Body body) {
```

```
      this.body = body;
    }

    @Override
    public Body getBody() {
      return body;
    }

    @Override
    public String getType() {
      return TYPE;
    }
  }
```

The getType() method returns a string, and we can choose any string as long as it is unique. The getBody() and setBody() methods are the getter and setter of the physics body. The Player class won't create the body itself. That is a job for the PlayerFactory class. Let's update it as well to deal with the physics. The following code snippet shows only the methods that have changed from the code in *Chapter 3, From Assets to Entities*:

```
  public class PlayerFactory {
    ...
    private PhysicsWorld physicsWorld;
    public static final FixtureDef PLAYER_FIXTURE =
      PhysicsFactory.createFixtureDef(1f, 0f, 1f, false);

    ...

    public void create(PhysicsWorld physicsWorld,
      VertexBufferObjectManager vbom) {
      this.physicsWorld = physicsWorld;
      this.vbom = vbom;
    }

    public Player createPlayer(float x, float y) {
      Player player = new Player(x, y,
        ResourceManager.getInstance().playerTextureRegion, vbom);
      player.setZIndex(2);

      Body playerBody = PhysicsFactory.createBoxBody(physicsWorld,
        player, BodyType.DynamicBody, PLAYER_FIXTURE);
      playerBody.setLinearDamping(1f);
      playerBody.setFixedRotation(true);
```

```
            playerBody.setUserData(player);
            physicsWorld.registerPhysicsConnector(new
               PhysicsConnector(player, playerBody));

            player.setBody(playerBody);
            return player;
         }

      @Override
      protected void onManagedUpdate(float pSecondsElapsed) {
         super.onManagedUpdate(pSecondsElapsed);
         if (getCurrentTileIndex() < 2) {
            if (body.getLinearVelocity().y < 0) {
               fall();
            } else {
               fly();
            }
         }
      }
   }
}
```

When creating the factory, the `PhysicsWorld` reference must be passed in. The factory needs it to create the body.

We are creating a dynamic body with one rectangular fixture using an AndEngine convenience method from the `PhysicsFactory` class. AndEngine measures the entity and then calls the appropriate Box2D method with the correct parameters.

The body will be exactly the same size as the player sprite. The fixture defines the body with density 1, no friction, and very bouncy. These parameters usually need some tweaking. Other parameters that we set are **linear damping** and fixed rotation. Damping can be both linear and angular, and it simply means that the body will slow down its movement as if going through a denser environment than vacuum, such as an atmosphere of water.

Finally, we set the user data of the body as our type, which we later use in collision handling, and register a connector between the body and the entity (the `Player` class). This means that the entity position (and rotation) will be updated by the body position (and rotation).

 Once the connector is created and registered, we should never set the position of the entity itself.

We have also added another option to change the look of our character based on the movement. In the same way we are making the character face left or right, we can change the currently-displayed sprite tile based on up and down movement. We can put this code in the GameScene class, but we can also encapsulate it in the player itself. That's what is happening here in the onManagedUpdate() method.

The last thing that remains is to change the GameScene code. We only need to pass the physics world to the PlayerFactory class. This can be done as follows:

```
public GameScene() {
  super();
  physicsWorld = new PhysicsWorld(new Vector2(0, -
    SensorManager.GRAVITY_EARTH), true);
  PlayerFactory.getInstance().create(physicsWorld, vbom);
}
```

If run now, the game will start with the player character in the middle of the screen slowly accelerating in the direction of the gravity.

Adding platforms

The next things we need in our game are platforms. We are going to create static and moving platforms. Our entity and factory model allows us to create only one class for both.

The Platform class belongs to the same package as the Player entity class. Its code is very simple:

```
public class Platform extends Sprite implements CollidableEntity {

  private Body body;

  public static final String TYPE = "Platform";

  public Platform(float pX, float pY,
    ITextureRegion pTextureRegion,
    VertexBufferObjectManager pVertexBufferObjectManager) {
    super(pX, pY, pTextureRegion, pVertexBufferObjectManager);
  }


  @Override
  protected void onManagedUpdate(float pSecondsElapsed) {
```

```
      super.onManagedUpdate(pSecondsElapsed);
    }

    @Override
    public void setBody(Body body) {
      this.body = body;
    }

    @Override
    public Body getBody() {
      return body;
    }

    @Override
    public String getType() {
      return TYPE;
    }
  }
```

The `Platform` class is based on the `Sprite` class and returns the type `Platform`. Other than that, we only implement the setter and getter for the body. Most of the interesting code is in the `PlatformFactory` class:

```
public class PlatformFactory {

  public static final FixtureDef PLATFORM_FIXTURE =
    PhysicsFactory.createFixtureDef(0f, 0f, 1f, false);

  private static PlatformFactory INSTANCE = new PlatformFactory();
  private PhysicsWorld physicsWorld;
  private VertexBufferObjectManager vbom;

  private PlatformFactory() {   }

  public static PlatformFactory getInstance() {
    return INSTANCE;
  }

  public void create(PhysicsWorld physicsWorld,
    VertexBufferObjectManager vbom) {
```

```
        this.physicsWorld = physicsWorld;
        this.vbom = vbom;
    }

    public Platform createPlatform(float x, float y) {
        Platform platform = new Platform(x, y,
            ResourceManager.getInstance().platformTextureRegion, vbom);
        platform.setAnchorCenterY(1);

        final float[] sceneCenterCoordinates =
            platform.getSceneCenterCoordinates();
        final float centerX =
            sceneCenterCoordinates[Constants.VERTEX_INDEX_X];
        final float centerY =
            sceneCenterCoordinates[Constants.VERTEX_INDEX_Y];

        Body platformBody = PhysicsFactory.createBoxBody(physicsWorld,
            centerX, centerY,
            platform.getWidth() - 20, 1,
            BodyType.KinematicBody, PLATFORM_FIXTURE);
        platformBody.setUserData(platform);
        physicsWorld.registerPhysicsConnector(new
            PhysicsConnector(platform, platformBody));
        platform.setBody(platformBody);
        return platform;
    }

    public Platform createMovingPlatform(float x, float y, float
        velocity) {
        Platform platform = createPlatform(x, y);
        platform.getBody().setLinearVelocity(velocity, 0);
        return platform;
    }
}
```

There are two methods: createPlatform() and createMovingPlatform(). The first one creates a static platform. We are using a kinematic body here, but it could be a static body as well. The reason is simply to save some lines of code. If our simulation had more bodies, it would be better to strictly use static bodies for static platforms and kinematic bodies for moving platforms. Static bodies need less processing time than kinematic ones. Using kinematic bodies could negatively influence the performance.

We are first creating a sprite and later adding a body that doesn't cover the full sprite, but in fact, it is just a thin line on top of the platform. We want only the top part of the platform to react to the collisions. The highlighted code in the previous code snippet is the easiest way to achieve this. The physics body-bounding boxes are shown as red rectangles in the following screenshot from the game:

Finally, we add the code to the GameScene class that will insert the platform into the game. For now, we are going to add just one static platform for the player to land on as shown in the previous screenshot. This can be done as follows:

```
Random rand = new Random();

private LinkedList<Platform> platforms = new
  LinkedList<Platform>();

public GameScene() {
  super();
  physicsWorld = new PhysicsWorld(new Vector2(0, -
    SensorManager.GRAVITY_EARTH), true);
  PlayerFactory.getInstance().create(physicsWorld, vbom);
```

```
        PlatformFactory.getInstance().create(physicsWorld, vbom);
    }

    @Override
    public void populate() {
        createBackground();
        createPlayer();
        createHUD();

        addPlatform(240, 50, false);

        engine.enableAccelerationSensor(activity, this);
        registerUpdateHandler(physicsWorld);
    }

    private void addPlatform(float tx, float ty, boolean moving) {
        Platform platform;
        if (moving) {
            platform = PlatformFactory.getInstance().createMovingPlatform
                (tx, ty, (rand.nextFloat() - 0.5f) * 10f);
        } else {
            platform = PlatformFactory.getInstance().createPlatform(tx,
                ty);
        }
        attachChild(platform);
        platforms.add(platform);
    }
```

We have added a random number generator to the GameScene class that is used in the addPlatform() method to randomly send a platform in a random direction. We also added a list of platforms because we will be adding and removing them dynamically as the player moves upwards.

We are creating the PlatformFactory class in the constructor and adding one platform in the populate() method using the addPlatform() method.

When the character falls on the platform, there is a little twitch when the two frames—fly and fall—are changing very quickly. This is expected because we did not implement the same threshold for up and down frames as we did for left and right. The character is almost unnoticeably bouncing for a short time, up and down. But, when we add a spring to the platform to propel the player upwards, the twitch will not happen.

Controlling the player character

The gravity vector is fixed and it is pointing down along the *y* axis of the device in portrait mode. There are no other forces in place, which means our character now falls straight down. We have several options on how to make the character move left and right using the Android device tilt. We already used the accelerometer readings and moved the character using the entity modifiers. Now, we will do the same using the physics engine.

Changing the gravity vector

The first option is to change the gravity vector based on the accelerometer readings. We only want to change the *x* axis movement, and the more the phone is tilted, the faster the character should move. Therefore, we will keep the vertical part of the vector and change only the horizontal part based on the accelerometer readings.

This is not the most realistic option, but it's the one that is the easiest and gives the best result.

The following code shows how it is done. Let's change the `onAccelerationChanged()` method.

```
float lastX = 0;
@Override
public void onAccelerationChanged(final AccelerationData
  pAccelerationData) {
  if (Math.abs(pAccelerationData.getX() - lastX) > 0.5) {
    if (pAccelerationData.getX() > 0) {
      player.turnRight();
    } else {
      player.turnLeft();
    }
    lastX = pAccelerationData.getX();
  }
  final Vector2 gravity =
    Vector2Pool.obtain(pAccelerationData.getX() * 8, -
    SensorManager.GRAVITY_EARTH * 4);
  this.physicsWorld.setGravity(gravity);
  Vector2Pool.recycle(gravity);
}
```

The highlighted code was added and it does three things. First, we obtain a vector object from a pool of objects. This is an optimization technique that prevents garbage collection.

Android is based on Java, and Java frees the memory by removing data that is no longer in use. This is called garbage collection, and it can cause short lags during gameplay. If we simply created a new vector here, a lot of objects would be created; one per accelerometer reading. This would cause garbage collection quite often. Therefore, it's better to reuse these objects. The pool contains a few objects that are reused and never garbage collected until the whole pool is discarded.

Secondly, the accelerometer's horizontal value is used as the new gravity horizontal part multiplied by a constant. We also multiply the y-value of gravity by a constant to make the fall faster and the game more action-packed.

Lastly, we return the used vector to the pool in order to recycle it. Because the values are set directly to the Box2D engine, we no longer need the vector object, but we want to make it available in future iterations with new values.

When we run the game now, the character falls down and the direction of the fall can be influenced by tilting the device. The black arrow in the following illustration shows the final direction (vector) of movement. When the device is tilted, the vector is composed of the original vertical value (red) and the new horizontal value (blue).

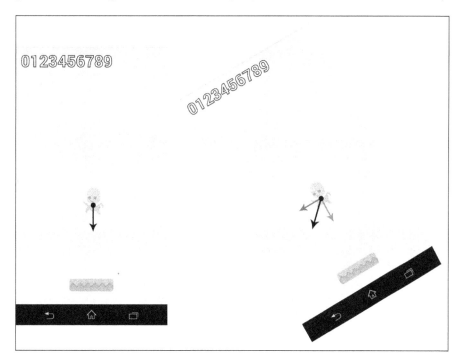

When the character lands on the platform and stops moving, it can no longer move at all no matter how much we tilt the device. This is because the character is asleep. It can only be awaken after another collision happens or a force is applied to it.

 When creating the physics world, we can turn sleeping on or off for all bodies. Each individual body also has a property called `sleepingAllowed` that can be set manually.

Using forces

Instead of changing the gravity vector, we can apply a force to the character as an alternative. We are not going to use this method in the end, but it can be useful in other cases. Using forces is the most realistic option.

Let's temporarily change the `onAccelerationChanged()` method in the `GameScene` class as follows:

```
public void onAccelerationChanged(final AccelerationData
  pAccelerationData) {
  if (Math.abs(pAccelerationData.getX() - lastX) > 0.5) {
    if (pAccelerationData.getX() > 0) {
      player.turnRight();
    } else {
      player.turnLeft();
    }
    lastX = pAccelerationData.getX();
  }
  final Vector2 force =
    Vector2Pool.obtain(pAccelerationData.getX() * 50, 0);
  final Vector2 point = player.getBody().getWorldCenter();
  player.getBody().applyForce(force, point);
  Vector2Pool.recycle(force);
}
```

The highlighted part has changed. Now, we first obtain a vector from the pool and set its horizontal value to the accelerometer's horizontal value multiplied by a big constant. We use the constant because we want to apply a force big enough to move our character. To accelerate the object faster, we need to use a bigger value. We should factor in the time between two accelerometer readings as well, but for simplicity, a constant will do.

We are also using the center of the player character as the point where we apply the force. The `Body` class has a method that returns the position of the center of gravity of the body in the physics world coordinates.

When we run the game now, the character's fall can again be influenced by tilting the device, but the final effect is different. It feels somehow lazier. This is due to the fact that the forces are applied gradually over time. When changing the direction, we must first overcome the character's inertia.

This method can be used to simulate a jet pack, because a jet pack would have exactly this kind of effect on the character.

Using impulses

Impulse is a force applied over time. When we call the `applyImpulse()` method, it has the same effect as if we have been applying a force over a period of time, but it is applied immediately.

We are going to change the code of the `onAccelerationChanged()` method once again. The difference from the last code is minimal, just two highlighted lines:

```
public void onAccelerationChanged(final AccelerationData
  pAccelerationData) {
  if (Math.abs(pAccelerationData.getX() - lastX) > 0.5) {
    if (pAccelerationData.getX() > 0) {
      player.turnRight();
    } else {
      player.turnLeft();
    }
    lastX = pAccelerationData.getX();
  }
  final Vector2 force =
    Vector2Pool.obtain(pAccelerationData.getX() * 5, 0);
  final Vector2 point = player.getBody().getWorldCenter();
  player.getBody().applyLinearImpulse(force, point);
  Vector2Pool.recycle(force);
}
```

We need to use a smaller value when applying the impulse, because its effect is stronger. Other than that, we only change one method for the other. When we run the game now, the character is going to change direction more quickly.

Setting the velocity directly

This method is not recommended. Setting the velocity directly can break the physics simulation, because it is something that doesn't happen naturally. On the other hand, when adding a new object to the simulation, setting its initial velocity might be what we need.

For one last time, we are going to change the onAccelerationChanged() method:

```
float lastX = 0;
@Override
public void onAccelerationChanged(final AccelerationData
  pAccelerationData) {
  if (Math.abs(pAccelerationData.getX() - lastX) > 0.5) {
    if (pAccelerationData.getX() > 0) {
      player.turnRight();
    } else {
      player.turnLeft();
    }
    lastX = pAccelerationData.getX();
  }
  final Vector2 velocity =
    Vector2Pool.obtain(pAccelerationData.getX() * 2,
    player.getBody().getLinearVelocity().y);
  player.getBody().setLinearVelocity(velocity);
  Vector2Pool.recycle(velocity);
}
```

In this case, we are creating the velocity vector using the horizontal value from the accelerometer and the vertical value from the body itself, set by the physics engine. While this certainly works, it doesn't happen naturally and it breaks the simulation too.

Summary

This chapter dealt with physics in AndEngine. Now, we know that AndEngine is using a port of a popular two-dimensional physics engine called Box2D. Basic terms such as force, impulse, velocity, fixture, restitution, friction, and density were explained. We learned the differences between bodies, their properties, and how the properties influence the final simulation.

In the second part, we added the engine to the game and implemented a way to control the character using tilt and physics. Multiple ways were discussed with their advantages and drawbacks.

In the next chapter, we will add enemies and work with collisions and game events. We will learn how to manipulate the physics bodies and add and remove platforms dynamically. We are also going to add enemies, and to make the game more interactive, we will add sounds to the collisions.

7
Detecting Collisions and Reacting to Events

In this chapter, we are going to add a physics-based collision detector to our game and create events based on the detected collisions. We are going to learn how to trigger events from different phases of a collision and for specific types of colliding bodies. We will also learn how to handle these collision events and many other events such as "game over".

Finally, we are going to learn how to play sound effects that we prepared earlier in the game during the events to improve their overall feel.

Collisions

Collisions are an integral part of the physics engine. Algorithms used in Box2D are nicely optimized and we will take advantage of it. However, we will be adding and removing physics bodies during the game because it's usually a good idea to keep the number of bodies to a minimum. Even the best algorithms will take some time to calculate all collisions and too many bodies might mean a significant slowdown.

While adding bodies is usually easy and can be done without any problem, removing bodies must be done at a specific time and it is one of the most common culprits of strange crashes in games with physics.

Detecting collisions

Collisions are detected automatically by Box2D, and collision events are handled in a **contact listener**. Here's an example of the simplest contact listener. Let's create a class called `MyContactListener` in the `is.kul.learningandengine.scene` package and let it implement the `ContactListener` interface:

```
public class MyContactListener implements ContactListener {

  Player player;

  public MyContactListener(Player player) {
    this.player = player;
  }

  @Override
  public void beginContact(Contact contact) {
  }

  @Override
  public void endContact(Contact contact) {
  }

  @Override
  public void preSolve(Contact contact, Manifold oldManifold) {
  }

  @Override
  public void postSolve(Contact contact, ContactImpulse impulse) {
  }
}
```

The `ContactListener` interface, like many other classes and interfaces in the physics extension, belongs to a `com.badlogic` package. This is due to the fact that AndEngine's physics extension is based on the libgdx physics library. libgdx is another popular Android game framework and can be found at `http://libgdx.badlogicgames.com/`.

The ContactListener interface contains the following four callback methods; each of them is called during a different phase of a contact:

- The beginContact method is called when two fixtures from two different bodies start to overlap. This is the place where we want to play a sound on impact, show explosion animation, and so on.

- The endContact method is called when two fixtures stop overlapping.

- The preSolve method is called after the collision is detected but before any calculation of the result is done. We are going to implement the one-sided platform by turning off the collision in this method.

- The postSolve method is called after all the collision calculations have been done. It is possible to access the final impulse that will be applied to the body.

The collision always starts with beginContact. Then, preSolve and postSolve are called, and they can be called multiple times if the contact is still in place. Finally, endContact is called.

> The physics world can't be manipulated inside the listener. For example, it would be a big mistake to destroy a body in the postSolve method because the processing would continue thinking that the body still exists. In AndEngine, such action usually results in an unexpected crash. The best practice in this case is to save the bodies that need to be manipulated to another temporary list and do so before the next Box2D step. One of the options is to use the runOnUpdateThread() method.

Our contact listener also keeps a reference to the player to be able to manipulate its speed. To enable our contact listener, we simply set it in our current physics world. We do this in the GameScene class in the populate() method, as follows:

```
@Override
public void populate() {
  createBackground();
  createPlayer();
  createHUD();

  addPlatform(240, 100, false);

  engine.enableAccelerationSensor(activity, this);
  registerUpdateHandler(physicsWorld);

  physicsWorld.setContactListener(new MyContactListener(player));
}
```

The player-platform collision

We will start with a simple player-platform collision. Right now in our game, there is just one platform and the player falling straight on it.

When the collision is detected, the `Contact` object is passed in the `beginContact()` method. Contact contains two fixtures that are overlapping. Each fixture belongs to a body so that we can check what kind of bodies are actually colliding.

 The order of bodies is not guaranteed. Always check whether it is *A* in contact with *B* or *B* with *A*.

Let's add a convenient method to `MyContactListener` to make distinguishing the collisions easier:

```
    private boolean checkContact(Contact contact, String typeA, String
typeB) {
        if (contact.getFixtureA().getBody().getUserData() instanceof
CollidableEntity &&
            contact.getFixtureB().getBody().getUserData() instanceof
CollidableEntity) {
            CollidableEntity ceA = (CollidableEntity) contact.getFixtureA().
getBody().getUserData();
            CollidableEntity ceB = (CollidableEntity) contact.getFixtureB().
getBody().getUserData();

            if (typeA.equals(ceA.getType()) && typeB.equals(ceB.getType())
||
                typeA.equals(ceB.getType()) && typeB.equals(ceA.getType()))
{
                return true;

            }
        }
        return false;
    }
```

We are making use of our `CollidableEntity` interface. If both fixtures belong to bodies that are a part of `CollidableEntities`, we can safely cast them to the `CollidableEntities` interface and then retrieve their type. In the branching statement, we first check whether `typeA` just collided with `typeB` or `typeB` with `typeA`.

Back in *Chapter 2, Game Concept and Assets,* we discussed the game rules. The platforms should be passable from bottom-up and solid when fell onto. Here's the illustration again:

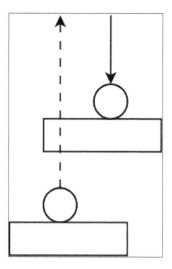

Moreover, on contact after the fall, the platform must propel the main character upwards. Here's how to achieve this behavior in the preSolve() method of MyContactListener:

```
@Override
public void preSolve(Contact contact, Manifold oldManifold) {
    if (checkContact(contact, Player.TYPE, Platform.TYPE)) {
      // player and platform
      if (!player.isDead() && player.getBody().getLinearVelocity().y <
0) {
        player.getBody().setLinearVelocity(new Vector2(0, 40));
      } else {
        contact.setEnabled(false);
      }
    }
}
```

First, we check whether the player is still alive. This check is important because we want a dead player to fall through any remaining platforms. Then, we check whether the player is currently falling by checking the vertical component of its linear velocity. If both conditions are true, we have a live player character falling on a platform and we propel it upwards. It other cases, we simply mark the contact as disabled, which has the same effect as if the contact never happened.

In this particular case, we are setting the velocity directly because we want to cancel all forces that could be influencing the player's character and propel it straight up with a given speed.

To illustrate this behavior a little bit better, let's add another platform above our first platform:

```
@Override
public void populate() {
...

    addPlatform(240, 100, false);
    addPlatform(340, 400, false);


...
  }
```

After running the game now, the player will fall on the first platform and it is propelled upwards. We can now tilt the device right and the player will move in the direction of the other platform. If it approaches from the bottom, it will pass through. If it falls on it, then it will be propelled upwards.

The player-enemy collision

It's time to add enemies to the game. Our enemy will be the animated fly, as shown in the following screenshot:

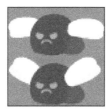

The Enemy class and EnemyFactory

The enemy entity will be represented by a new class called `Enemy` and will be created by a new factory called `EnemyFactory`. We will put these classes into their respective packages:

```
public class Enemy extends AnimatedSprite implements CollidableEntity
{
```

```
    public static final String TYPE = "ENEMY";

    private Body body;

    public Enemy(float pX, float pY,
        ITiledTextureRegion pTiledTextureRegion,
        VertexBufferObjectManager pVertexBufferObjectManager) {
      super(pX, pY, pTiledTextureRegion, pVertexBufferObjectManager);
    }

    @Override
    public void setBody(Body body) {
      this.body = body;
    }

    @Override
    public Body getBody() {
      return body;
    }

    @Override
    public String getType() {
      return TYPE;
    }
  }
```

The class is not much different from the platform class. The only important difference is TYPE being set to ENEMY and that the extended class is AnimatedSprite in this case.

The factory for enemies follows the same pattern as our other factories.
Here's the code:

```
public class EnemyFactory {
  public static final FixtureDef ENEMY_FIXTURE = PhysicsFactory.
createFixtureDef(1f, 0f, 1f, true);

  private static EnemyFactory INSTANCE = new EnemyFactory();
  private PhysicsWorld physicsWorld;
  private VertexBufferObjectManager vbom;

  private EnemyFactory() {  }
```

```
  public static EnemyFactory getInstance() {
    return INSTANCE;
  }


  public void create(PhysicsWorld physicsWorld,
VertexBufferObjectManager vbom) {
    this.physicsWorld = physicsWorld;
    this.vbom = vbom;
  }


  public Enemy createEnemy(float x, float y) {
    Enemy enemy = new Enemy(x, y, ResourceManager.getInstance().
enemyTextureRegion, vbom);

    Body enemyBody = PhysicsFactory.createBoxBody(physicsWorld, enemy,
        BodyType.KinematicBody, ENEMY_FIXTURE);

    enemyBody.setUserData(enemy);
    physicsWorld.registerPhysicsConnector(new PhysicsConnector(enemy,
enemyBody));

    enemy.setBody(enemyBody);
    enemyBody.setLinearVelocity(-1, 0);
    enemy.animate(75);
    enemy.setZIndex(1);
    return enemy;
  }
}
```

Again, we use a single instance of this factory. We need a method to return the
single instance and a method to create the factory itself. Lastly, we need a method
to create enemies. We have seen all this code before. The only difference here is that
we are calling the `animate()` method to animate the fly — change frames each 75
milliseconds and we set the enemy to move with a small velocity leftwards.

Adding enemies to the scene

As we will be adding enemies to the scene as the view moves upwards and
removing them as they disappear at the bottom edge of the display, we are
going to need the following changes to the `GameScene` class. The changes are
highlighted in the following code:

```
    private LinkedList<Enemy> enemies = new LinkedList<Enemy>();

    public GameScene() {
```

```
    super();
    physicsWorld = new PhysicsWorld(new Vector2(0, -SensorManager.
GRAVITY_EARTH * 4), true);
    PlayerFactory.getInstance().create(physicsWorld, vbom);
    PlatformFactory.getInstance().create(physicsWorld, vbom);
    EnemyFactory.getInstance().create(physicsWorld, vbom);
}

private void addEnemy(float tx, float ty) {
    Enemy enemy = EnemyFactory.getInstance().createEnemy(tx, ty);
    attachChild(enemy);
    enemies.add(enemy);
}

@Override
public void populate() {
    createBackground();
    createPlayer();
    createHUD();

    addPlatform(240, 100, false);
    addPlatform(340, 400, false);
    addEnemy(140, 400);

    engine.enableAccelerationSensor(activity, this);
    registerUpdateHandler(physicsWorld);

    physicsWorld.setContactListener(new
MyContactListener(player));
}
```

First, we need to create the enemy factory in the constructor to make sure that it is available later. The addEnemy() method simply adds the fly at the correct position, and in the populate() method, we are insert one of the enemies.

Updating the contact listener

Finally, we update the contact listener. It is very simple and is as follows:

```
@Override
public void beginContact(Contact contact) {
    if (checkContact(contact, Player.TYPE, Enemy.TYPE)) {
        player.die();
    }
}
```

After collision is detected, we check whether it is a collision between the player and the enemy, and if yes, we mark the player as dead. This will switch the frame of the player and also stop it from colliding with platforms. It will fall off the screen.

This concludes the part about collisions. We are now ready to move the camera and add and remove platforms.

Game events

There are a handful of events that we need to handle: the player jumps out of the screen, a new platform or enemy is added, a platform or enemy is removed, and a player dies. The player's character can die in two ways: when it collides with the enemy, which we already implemented, and when it falls off the screen. We also want to reward the player with a score when he or she reaches a new height.

There is one more special event we need to cover. When the player's character exits the screen on the left or right side, we want it to reappear on the other side. We want to create a wrapped world. Same with platforms and later enemies when we make them move.

The chase camera

When the camera is following the main character, it is called a chase camera in AndEngine. Any camera can be chasing any entity by simply calling the following function:

```
camera.setChaseEntity(entity);
```

However, in our case, this is not exactly what we want. We need the camera to follow only the upward movement of the player when it is alive and downward when it dies.

For our purpose, we are going to create a new camera class that will inherit the functionality from AndEngine's SmoothCamera. This type of camera moves smoothly from one point to another when a new position is set. We will implement our own chasing and restrict it to the vertical movement. Create a new class called MyCamera in the is.kul.learningandengine package, as shown in the following code:

```
public class MyCamera extends SmoothCamera {

    private IEntity chaseEntity;
```

```
    private boolean gameOver = false;

    public MyCamera(float pX, float pY, float pWidth, float pHeight) {
        super(pX, pY, pWidth, pHeight, 3000f, 1000f, 1f);
    }

    @Override
    public void setChaseEntity(IEntity pChaseEntity) {
        super.setChaseEntity(pChaseEntity);
        this.chaseEntity = pChaseEntity;
    }

    @Override
    public void updateChaseEntity() {
        if (chaseEntity != null) {
            if (chaseEntity.getY() > getCenterY()) {
                setCenter(getCenterX(), chaseEntity.getY());
            } else if (chaseEntity.getY() < getYMin() && !gameOver) {
                setCenter(getCenterX(), chaseEntity.getY() - getHeight());
                gameOver = true;
            }
        }
    }
}
```

The constructor calls the SmoothCamera constructor to set fast, but still smooth zooming. The two large number parameters are pixel per second and maximal velocities, and the last parameter is zoom velocity, which we are not going to use.

We are implementing our own chase entity logic, and as the chase entity is hidden from its children in other camera classes, we have to implement the setter as well. We are overriding the updateChaseEntity method to create the behavior we need. The first branch of the if statement checks whether the character moved upwards. The second branch checks for the falling. If the character falls beyond the lower bounds of the camera, the camera automatically centers to the character once, which looks like the camera is following it for a while. Afterwards, the chasing stops and character falls off the screen. In fact, the camera stops following the character immediately when it dies, and the single smooth shift to the character's location creates the nice effect.

To use our camera, we need to update two classes. First, the `GameActivity` class:

```
@Override
public EngineOptions onCreateEngineOptions() {
   Camera camera = new MyCamera(0, 0, CAMERA_WIDTH, CAMERA_HEIGHT);
...
   }
```

Then update the `GameScene` class:

```
@Override
public void populate() {
   createBackground();
   createPlayer();
   camera.setChaseEntity(player);
   createHUD();

...
   }
```

Adding and removing platforms and enemies

Now that our camera follows the character, it's time to start adding platforms and removing the platforms that are no longer visible. Thanks to the special camera, we are sure that a platform that leaves the screen will never appear again and thus can be safely removed.

Here's a basic idea of what we want to achieve. The arrow shows the direction that the world, and therefore the platforms, move:

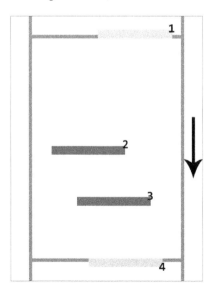

As the player moves up, we will have to add a new platform. We are going to check the distance between the uppermost platform (**2**) and the upper bound of the current camera view (**1**). If the distance reaches a certain threshold, we are going to add a new platform and the position (**1**).

We will also check the position of the lowermost platform (**3**). When it reaches the lower bounds of the current camera view (**4**), we are going to remove this platform.

Enemies work exactly the same way. We will make use of it and add and remove them together with platforms.

First, we add a method to the GameScene class that removes all unwanted entities in a list. Here's what it looks like:

```
    private void cleanEntities(List<? extends CollidableEntity> list,
float bound) {
      Iterator<? extends CollidableEntity> iter = list.iterator();
      while (iter.hasNext()) {
        CollidableEntity ce = iter.next();
          if (ce.getY() < bound) {
            iter.remove();
            ce.detachSelf();
            physicsWorld.destroyBody(ce.getBody());
          }
      }
    }
```

This method simply iterates over all entities in a list, and if their *y* coordinate is lower than the specified bound, the entity is removed from the list, the sprite is detached from the scene, and the physics body is destroyed.

Secondly, we override the onManagedUpdate() method to calculate when to add entities and call the cleanEntities() method:

```
    private static final float MIN = 50f;
    private static final float MAX = 250f;

    @Override
    protected void onManagedUpdate(float pSecondsElapsed) {
      super.onManagedUpdate(pSecondsElapsed);
      boolean added = false;
      while (camera.getYMax() > platforms.getLast().getY()) {
        // x position of next platform
        float tx = rand.nextFloat() * GameActivity.CAMERA_WIDTH;
        // y position of next platform
        float ty = platforms.getLast().getY() + MIN + rand.nextFloat() *
(MAX - MIN);
        // 10 % chance to add enemy on the platform
```

```
        if (rand.nextFloat() < 0.1) {
          addEnemy(tx, ty);
        }
        boolean moving = rand.nextBoolean();
        addPlatform(tx, ty, moving);
        added = true;
      }
      if (added) {
        sortChildren();
      }
      cleanEntities(platforms, camera.getYMin());
      cleanEntities(enemies, camera.getYMin());
    }
```

The first two lines are the minimum and maximum distance between platforms in pixels. The method itself first defines a Boolean variable called `added` that is set to `true` if anything was added and we need to sort the children of the scene. This is important because we set the z-indexes of all entities to keep the player on top and we must resort to everything whenever we add an entity.

Next, we calculate whether we need to add a platform. This happens whenever the distance between the top bound of the camera view is higher than the topmost platform. We also add a new enemy on a platform with 10 percent chance.

Finally, we call the `cleanEntities()` method on both platforms and enemies to clean any entities that are below the visible area. We should see something like this in the game now; multiple platforms and enemies here and there:

Detecting the player character's death

Detecting the player character's death is in fact very simple. The only thing we need is add the following code to the onManagedUpdate() method:

```
// player below last platform
if (player.getY() < platforms.getFirst().getY()) {
  player.die();
}
```

If the player happens to be below the last platform, the game is over. When the main character dies, it stops colliding with platforms (also there are no more platforms) and falls down.

Score

There are few things that can serve as a score in your game. It can be the number of platforms reached or height reached. Let's make it simple and say that the score will be the maximum number of pixels that the lower bound of the camera has reached. This is not only easy to implement but will also secure a lot of points.

First, we add a score counter, and then, we add a method that will increase the counter every time the camera moves. The new code is highlighted and only the relevant part in onManagedUpdate() is shown:

```
private int score;

    private void createHUD() {
    HUD hud = new HUD();
    scoreText = new Text(16, 784, res.font, "0123456789", new
TextOptions(HorizontalAlign.LEFT), vbom);
    scoreText.setAnchorCenter(0, 1);
    score = 0;
    scoreText.setText(String.valueOf(score));
    hud.attachChild(scoreText);
    camera.setHUD(hud);
  }

  @Override
  protected void onManagedUpdate(float pSecondsElapsed) {
...

    calculateScore();
  }
```

```
private void calculateScore() {
  if (camera.getYMin() > score) {
    score = Math.round(camera.getYMin());
    scoreText.setText(String.valueOf(score));
  }

}
```

The score is calculated from the number of the pixels of the camera's lower vertical bound. We have to use rounding because the bound can actually be a floating point number.

When we run the game now, the score starts increasing very fast as soon as the player starts moving upwards.

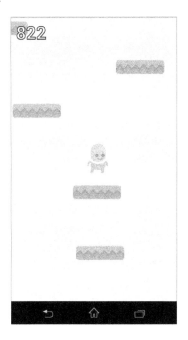

Wrapping the world around

The game almost works. It is possible to jump up, die from falling, and die from touching the enemy. However, when the character leaves the screen left or right, it is lost. There are also moving platforms that move outside the view and never come back. Moreover, we would like to have moving enemies because now they simply sit on platforms, making it almost impossible to use such a platform.

The solution to all these problems is a **wraparound**. When anything leaves the screen on the left (or right), it should reappear on the right (or left) again. We can imagine this as if the screen was actually wrapped around a cylinder.

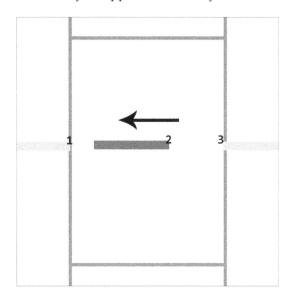

The easiest way to create a wraparound is to move the object that completely left the screen on one side to the other side. Some variants of wraparound work in another way. The object that starts leaving immediately appears on the other side, so at a certain time, we can see it on both sides. However, such a wraparound is not as simple to create, and therefore, we will implement only the easy solution.

The solution is the same for all our moving entities, but we can't add the same functionality to the common ancestor without changing the AndEngine code. Therefore, we will create a simple utility class that will contain one method called wraparound().

Let's create it in the is.kul.learningandengine.entity package and call it Utils:

```
public class Utils {
  public static void wraparound(CollidableEntity ce) {

    if (ce.getX() + ce.getWidth() / 2 < 0) {
      ce.getBody().setTransform((GameActivity.CAMERA_WIDTH +
ce.getWidth() / 2) / PhysicsConstants.PIXEL_TO_METER_RATIO_DEFAULT,
          ce.getBody().getPosition().y, 0);
    } else if (ce.getX() - ce.getWidth() / 2 > GameActivity.CAMERA_
WIDTH) {
      ce.getBody().setTransform((- ce.getWidth() / 2) /
PhysicsConstants.PIXEL_TO_METER_RATIO_DEFAULT,
```

```
            ce.getBody().getPosition().y, 0);
        }
      }
    }
```

The method checks whether the right bound of the object exited the left side, or the left bound of the object exited the right side of the screen. In both the cases, the code teleports the object to the other side without changing its speed. Therefore, platforms keep moving in the correct direction, the player keeps falling, and so on.

To use this wraparound feature, we must add it to the onManagedUpdate() method of each entity. In the case of the Player class, we add it to the existing code, as follows:

```
@Override
protected void onManagedUpdate(float pSecondsElapsed) {
  super.onManagedUpdate(pSecondsElapsed);
  Utils.wraparound(this);
  // if somebody set we are dying, we can't switch anymore
  if (getCurrentTileIndex() < 2) {
    if (body.getLinearVelocity().y < 0) {
      fall();
    } else {
      fly();
    }
  }
}
```

For both Platform and Enemy, we need to override the method, as follows:

```
@Override
protected void onManagedUpdate(float pSecondsElapsed) {
  super.onManagedUpdate(pSecondsElapsed);
  Utils.wraparound(this);
}
```

Restarting the game after a player dies

The only thing remaining now is to show some kind of end screen with the score and allow the player to restart the game.

The way we implemented it, the player can die in two ways. First, when the player touches the enemy and secondly when the player falls under the last platform. This presents us with a common problem: how do we know that the game has finished? Fortunately, we have added the dead field to the Player class, so we can always know whether the player is alive or dead.

There are more solutions to this problem. Another solution is to have a method accessible from both the `MyContactListener` and `GameScene` classes that we can call on the player's death. However, that will introduce more **coupling** between the classes, which means that the classes will be more dependent on each other.

The best solution is probably to implement a **state machine**. Having different states for player alive, game paused, player dead, and so on. Our game is too simple and doesn't need a state machine yet. However, in *Chapter 10, Polishing the Game*, we are going to use a state machine to indicate which scene is currently active to show how it works. For now, a simple check will be enough.

Showing a message on game over

Let's start with showing a message to the player that the game is over. We want to add the message to the HUD, so that it won't move when the camera moves. Therefore, we change the `createHUD()` method in `GameScene` like this:

```
private Text endGameText;

private void createHUD() {
HUD hud = new HUD();
scoreText = new Text(16, 784, res.font, "0123456789", new
TextOptions(HorizontalAlign.LEFT), vbom);
scoreText.setAnchorCenter(0, 1);
score = 0;
scoreText.setText(String.valueOf(score));
hud.attachChild(scoreText);

endGameText = new Text(GameActivity.CAMERA_WIDTH / 2,
GameActivity.CAMERA_HEIGHT / 2,
    res.font, "GAME OVER! TAP TO CONTINUE", new
TextOptions(HorizontalAlign.CENTER), vbom);
endGameText.setAutoWrap(AutoWrap.WORDS);
endGameText.setAutoWrapWidth(300f);
endGameText.setVisible(false);
hud.attachChild(endGameText);

camera.setHUD(hud);
}
```

The added code creates a text entity that says Game over! Tap to continue. Next, we set **autowrap** of the text to AutoWrap.WORDS and limit the text to 300 pixels of width. This means that the text will automatically continue to the next line if it can't fit in 300 pixels, and words will be never be broken. The other option is AutoWrap.LETTERS, where the wrapping can break a word. There is a third option called AutoWrap.CJK, which is only useful for Asian characters such as Chinese, Korean, and Japanese. These languages have special line breaking rules. For example, certain characters might not come at the end of the line. We also set the visibility of this text to false to keep it hidden at the beginning.

Creating a hidden entity is a neat trick to show something quickly without running into problems with lags.

To show the text at the right time, we simply add the following code to the onManagedUpdate() method in GameScene:

```
if (player.isDead()) {
    endGameText.setVisible(true);
}
```

This will be called in every cycle of the game, which means up to 60 times per second. Fortunately, a simple "if" statement is very fast and won't negatively influence the game's speed.

This is how the message should look:

Restarting the game on tap

Next, we add a touch listener that will restart the game. There are basically two ways of performing a restart. A simple way is to destroy the whole scene and create everything again. A more complex way is to destroy and recreate all entities while keeping the scene.

We will use the latter. Creating the scene from scratch is basically the same as changing it, which we are going to do in *Chapter 9, Adding a Menu and Splash Scene*.

To remove all entities and restart the scene, we have to first implement the following method to the `MyCamera` class:

```
@Override
public void reset() {
  super.reset();
  gameOver = false;
  set(0, 0, GameActivity.CAMERA_WIDTH,
GameActivity.CAMERA_HEIGHT);
    setCenterDirect(GameActivity.CAMERA_WIDTH / 2,
GameActivity.CAMERA_HEIGHT / 2);
  }
```

This will set the camera to the same settings as when we created the camera anew. We set the `gameOver` flag to `false`, set the current camera view to the initial screen, and then use the `setCenterDirect()` method to stop any smooth movement of the camera that might be in progress.

Next, we will add the `restartGame()` method to the `GameScene` class:

```
private void restartGame() {
  setIgnoreUpdate(true);
  unregisterUpdateHandler(physicsWorld);
  enemies.clear();
  platforms.clear();
  physicsWorld.clearForces();
  physicsWorld.clearPhysicsConnectors();
  while (physicsWorld.getBodies().hasNext()) {
    physicsWorld.destroyBody(
physicsWorld.getBodies().next());
  }
  camera.reset();
  camera.setHUD(null);
  camera.setChaseEntity(null);
```

Detecting Collisions and Reacting to Events

```
    detachChildren();

    populate();
    setIgnoreUpdate(false);
}
```

This code first stops any updates from happening. This pauses the game and physics engine to allow us to manipulate it. Then, we unregister the physics world as a listener because we are going to register it again later. We clear the lists of platform and enemies, remove all forces and physics connectors from the physics world, and destroy all bodies.

Then, we reset the camera using the method we implemented earlier, remove its HUD and chase entity, and finally detach all entities from the GameScene class. Lastly, we call the populate method again and start updates again.

Finally, let's add the touch event listener and call the restartGame method on tap. We first make the GameScene class implement the IOnSceneTouchListener method and then implement the onSceneTouchEvent() method the following way (only the new method is shown):

```
public class GameScene extends AbstractScene implements
IAccelerationListener, IOnSceneTouchListener {
...
  @Override
  public boolean onSceneTouchEvent(Scene pScene, TouchEvent
pSceneTouchEvent) {
    if (pSceneTouchEvent.isActionUp() && player.isDead()) {
        restartGame();
      return true;
    }
    return false;
  }
}
```

We first check whether the touch happened after the player's death and then call the restartGame() method. This is everything that needs to be done to restart the game.

Playing sounds on events

The last thing that remains to be done to make the events feel more lively and real is to add sounds. We have prepared two sounds that we will play.

Just to refresh our memories, this is how we loaded the sounds in the
`ResourceManager` class:

```
public class ResourceManager {
  ...
  //sounds
  public Sound soundFall;
  public Sound soundJump;
  ...
  public void loadGameAudio() {
    try {
      SoundFactory.setAssetBasePath("sfx/");
      soundJump = SoundFactory.createSoundFromAsset(activity.
getSoundManager(), activity, "jump.ogg");
      soundFall = SoundFactory.createSoundFromAsset(activity.
getSoundManager(), activity, "fall.ogg");

      MusicFactory.setAssetBasePath("mfx/");
      music = MusicFactory.createMusicFromAsset(activity.
getMusicManager(), activity, "music.ogg");
    } catch (Exception e) {
      throw new RuntimeException("Error while loading audio", e);
    }
  }
  ...
}
```

Playing the jump sound

The jump sound should happen on the player-platform contact. Therefore, we are
going to play it in the `MyContactListener` class. Let's change the `preSolve()`
method like this:

```
@Override
public void preSolve(Contact contact, Manifold oldManifold) {
  if (checkContact(contact, Player.TYPE, Platform.TYPE)) {
    // player and platform
    if (!player.isDead() && player.getBody().getLinearVelocity().y <
0) {
      player.getBody().setLinearVelocity(new Vector2(0, 40));
      ResourceManager.getInstance().soundJump.play();
    } else {
      contact.setEnabled(false);
    }
  }
}
```

Playing a single sound is really just this simple.

Playing the fall sound when the player's character dies

Like with the jump sound, we only need very simple code. This time, we should play it when the player's death occurs. We can put this code to the `Player` class in the `die()` method as follows:

```
public void die() {
  if (!dead) {
    ResourceManager.getInstance().soundFall.play();
  }
  setDead(true);
  setCurrentTileIndex(2);
}
```

We are using an extra `if` statement that checks whether this is the first time the sound should play. If we haven't done this, the sound can be played multiple times, for example, when the player touches an enemy and then falls.

Summary

In this chapter, we have learned three seemingly unrelated concepts that help us to detect and react to events.

First, we added physics collisions to the game, and now we know how to use the collision listeners to both perform an action on collision and to ignore a collision. Secondly, we have identified basic events that happen throughout the game, on collisions, or simple in time, and we learned when and how to react to them. Lastly, we learned how to play sound effects on different events happening in different places.

In the next chapter, we are going to see some advanced physics such as multiple fixtures, joints, and collision filtering. The chapter will improve the look and feel (UX) of our game.

8
Advanced Physics

The gameplay of the game is almost complete, and we will take a short break from the game now. This chapter deals with a slightly more advanced topic, the advanced physics. While it is not necessary to add any of the concepts we are going to learn in this chapter to our game, they certainly can make the game's look and feel much better.

In this chapter, we will learn how to assemble bodies from multiple fixtures that will allow us to create more precise simulation, especially when it comes to collisions. We will also learn about joints, which are used to create systems of linked bodies and collision filtering. This will either help us to reduce the number of collisions, filter the unwanted collisions, and is also used to reduce the performance requirements.

We will use the current code from *Chapter 7, Detecting Collisions and Reacting to Events*, but we will add a lot of new things simply to illustrate the physics concepts. Therefore, most of the code will not be used in the final game. As this chapter is considered for advanced users and because the code is not essential for the game, this chapter can be skipped.

The Box2D Debug Draw extension

When working with simple physics, one can easily imagine how the bodies look and where the collisions happen. However, with added complexity, when a problem arises, it is almost impossible to find out where it lies without visual aid. This is where the Debug Draw extension comes in. Most of the Box2D ports will have a functionality to visualize the bodies using outlines and colors.

Such a visualization typically looks something like this:

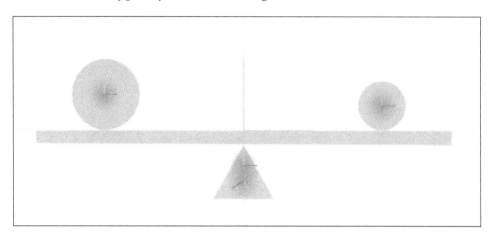

Adding Debug Draw to our AndEngine project

AndEngine has a Debug Draw extension as well. It was created by Nazgee, an AndEngine user and game programmer. It is an unofficial extension, but it works very well. It can be downloaded and added to any AndEngine project using the same method described in the *Downloading the sources* and *Adding AndEngine to Eclipse IDE* sections of *Chapter 1, Setting Up an AndEngine Project*, for the Box2D Physics Extension.

Here's the link to the original repository of the Debug Draw extension:

`https://github.com/nazgee/AndEngineDebugDrawExtension`

Here's an alternative link that is guaranteed to work with the source code of this book:

`https://github.com/sm4/AndEngineDebugDrawExtension`

This is, again, an optional part of the tutorial and not necessary to finish the game. However, it is very useful for any physics-based games with complex physics.

Using Debug Draw in a game

To use the Debug Draw extension, we only need to add the `DebugRenderer` object to our game. We can add it in the `GameScene` class in the `populate()` method:

```
DebugRenderer dr = new DebugRenderer(physicsWorld, vbom);
dr.setZIndex(999);
attachChild(dr);
```

The `DebugRenderer` object needs the `physicsWorld` handle and `vbom` (**Vertex Buffer Object Manager**). When it is attached to the scene, it reads all bodies from the physics world and renders them as colored outlines. The dynamic bodies are green, kinematic bodies are white, and static bodies are cyan. If a body sleeps, it is rendered as red and if it is not active, it is rendered with a black outline. Sensors are rendered as pink outlines and all joints have white outlines, as we are going to see later.

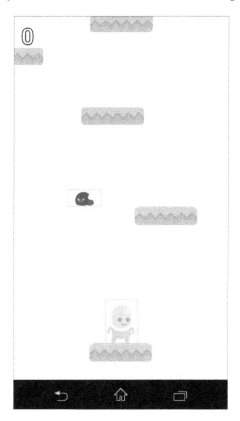

Assembling bodies from fixtures

So far, we have only used the AndEngine class, `PhysicsFactory`, to create rectangle (box) bodies. It is the simplest and most straightforward way to create bodies. The whole creation of a body remains hidden.

A body consists of one or more fixtures. Let's create a slightly more complicated body by manually creating three fixtures and putting them together to form a body. We will first create fixtures for the head, torso, and body, just to illustrate how to create multiple fixtures, but we are going to see how filtering works on the example of these fixtures as well.

 There are more ways of creating fixtures. One of the more automated ways is to use an external editor such as R.U.B.E. and a loader that will load the data to AndEngine. However, such a loader exists only as an unofficial extension.

Here's a screenshot showing how the final body should look in the game:

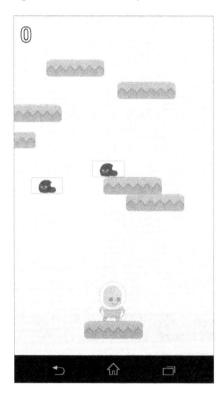

Creating an empty body

First, we need to create an empty body. The body is in fact just a virtual holder for fixtures. When we create an empty body and add it to the game, nothing will show and no collisions will happen. We are going to change the createPlayer() method of the PlayerFactory class. Here's the new code:

```
public Player createPlayer(float x, float y) {
    Player player = new Player(x, y, ResourceManager.getInstance().
playerTextureRegion, vbom);
    player.setZIndex(2);

    BodyDef bodyDef = new BodyDef();
    bodyDef.type = BodyType.DynamicBody;
    bodyDef.position.x = x / PhysicsConstants.PIXEL_TO_METER_RATIO_
DEFAULT;
    bodyDef.position.y = y / PhysicsConstants.PIXEL_TO_METER_RATIO_
DEFAULT;

    Body playerBody = physicsWorld.createBody(bodyDef);

    playerBody.setLinearDamping(1f);
    playerBody.setFixedRotation(true);
    playerBody.setUserData(player);
    physicsWorld.registerPhysicsConnector(new PhysicsConnector(player,
playerBody));

    player.setBody(playerBody);
    return player;
}
```

We are defining a BodyDef object that has a position. In the physics world, the units are meters, not pixels. Therefore, we use the pixel-to-meter conversion. We specified that our BodyDef object defines a dynamic body. Other than this, we keep the code unchanged. Next, we are going to add the fixtures. Each fixture can have different properties. Let's make use of that.

The head fixture

What we want to achieve is almost perfect collisions with the enemy flies. Moreover, right now, the whole body collides with a platform, making it jump even when the head touches it, and this is something we don't really want. Only the legs should propel the player upwards. What we can do is to turn the head into a circular shape sensor.

Sensors do not generate the pre-solve and post-solve events in the contact listener. This makes sense because a sensor can't influence its environment; it's immaterial. However, it will still generate the begin and end contact events that we use to detect the contact with enemies.

Here's a method that will create a circular fixture where the player's head should be. It belongs to the `PlayerFactory` class:

```
    private void createHead(Body body) {
        FixtureDef headFixtureDef = PhysicsFactory.createFixtureDef(1f,
0f, 1f, true);
        CircleShape circle = new CircleShape();
        circle.setRadius(32 / PhysicsConstants.PIXEL_TO_METER_RATIO_
DEFAULT);
        circle.setPosition(new Vector2(0, 12 / PhysicsConstants.PIXEL_TO_
METER_RATIO_DEFAULT));
        headFixtureDef.shape = circle;
        body.createFixture(headFixtureDef);
    }
```

First, we create a fixture definition in the same way we created it before. Then, we create a circle shape, set its radius in meters, and set its position to the place where the character's head is, again in meters. Then, we assign this shape to the fixture definition and call the correct method in the `Body` class to create the fixture itself.

Before we add it to the final physics body, let's create the other fixtures as well.

Creating the torso

Circle shapes are easy; they only have a radius and position. To create every other shape, a polygon shape must be created. Polygons are tricky. They must be defined by vertices. Only convex polygon shapes are allowed; therefore, other shapes must be assembled from multiple fixtures. The order of vertices is defined by a simple rule. The "outside" of the shape is always on the right of each side. This means we have to define our vertices in a counterclockwise order, as shown in the following diagram:

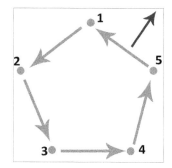

 Creating the vertices in the wrong order or creating a non-convex (concave) shape will most likely make the game crash with an error.

Creating the vertices manually is a bit tedious. Let's see how it looks for our trapezoid-shaped torso:

```
private void createTorso(Body body) {
    FixtureDef torsoFixtureDef = PhysicsFactory.createFixtureDef(1f,
0f, 0.5f, true);

    PolygonShape middleBox = new PolygonShape();

    final float halfWidth = 30 / PhysicsConstants.PIXEL_TO_METER_
RATIO_DEFAULT;
    final float halfHeight = 8 / PhysicsConstants.PIXEL_TO_METER_
RATIO_DEFAULT;
    final float yShift =  - 30 / PhysicsConstants.PIXEL_TO_METER_
RATIO_DEFAULT;
    Vector2[] vertices = new Vector2[4];
    vertices[0] = new Vector2(halfWidth, halfHeight + yShift);
    vertices[1] = new Vector2(-halfWidth, halfHeight + yShift);
    vertices[2] = new Vector2(-halfWidth * 0.75f, -halfHeight +
yShift);
    vertices[3] = new Vector2(halfWidth * 0.75f, -halfHeight +
yShift);
    middleBox.set(vertices);

    torsoFixtureDef.shape = middleBox;

    body.createFixture(torsoFixtureDef);
  }
```

The code is not complicated, just long. First, we create the fixture definition and again we want the torso to actually be a sensor. We create a `PolygonShape` object and set four vertices to it. The positions are defined using variables called `halfWidth` and `halfHeight`, so we can easily change all vertices at once. The following figure explains what they mean:

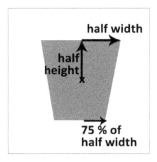

The following diagram shows the final points that are plotted:

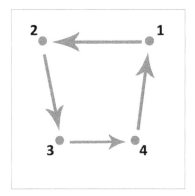

Creating the legs

Finally, we create the legs. We will use the same method using the polygonal shape as we used when creating the torso. However, this time we will create a rectangle, and we can use a convenience method, `setAsBox()`, to define the vertices for us.

Also, we don't want the legs to be a sensor, but rather a regular material part of the body. We are also going to increase the density of the legs to make the final body about the same weight as the original big box. This can be done as follows:

```
private void createLegs(Body body) {
    FixtureDef legsFixtureDef = PhysicsFactory.createFixtureDef(4f,
0.2f, 1f, false);
```

```
PolygonShape legsBox = new PolygonShape();
legsBox.setAsBox(20 / PhysicsConstants.PIXEL_TO_METER_RATIO_
DEFAULT,
      4 / PhysicsConstants.PIXEL_TO_METER_RATIO_DEFAULT,
      new Vector2(0, -44 / PhysicsConstants.PIXEL_TO_METER_RATIO_
DEFAULT),
          0);
legsFixtureDef.shape = legsBox;

body.createFixture(legsFixtureDef);
}
```

 There is a special polygonal shape—the edge. It is simply one edge of a polygon defined by two vertices. There is a method, `setAsEdge()`, to create this polygonal shape.

Assembling the body

Finally, we assemble the body parts together. This is done in the `createPlayer()` method in the `PlayerFactory` class, the same place where we created the empty body. We simply call the three methods that we just defined, as follows:

```
public Player createPlayer(float x, float y) {
    Player player = new Player(x, y, ResourceManager.getInstance().
playerTextureRegion, vbom);
    player.setZIndex(2);

    BodyDef bodyDef = new BodyDef();
    bodyDef.type = BodyType.DynamicBody;
    bodyDef.position.x = x / PhysicsConstants.PIXEL_TO_METER_RATIO_
DEFAULT;
    bodyDef.position.y = y / PhysicsConstants.PIXEL_TO_METER_RATIO_
DEFAULT;

    Body playerBody = physicsWorld.createBody(bodyDef);

    createTorso(playerBody);
    createHead(playerBody);
    createLegs(playerBody);

    playerBody.setLinearDamping(1f);
    playerBody.setFixedRotation(true);
    playerBody.setUserData(player);
```

```
    physicsWorld.registerPhysicsConnector(new PhysicsConnector(player,
playerBody));

    player.setBody(playerBody);
    return player;
}
```

We can run the game now. It will work almost the same as before, just with more precise collisions and the jumping will only happen when the player actually touches the platform top with legs.

Collision filtering

When we want two objects to pass each other, we can define them as never colliding with each other or even never colliding with anything. This is done by collision filtering. Each fixture can have the following three parameters defined:

- Its own category
- Other categories that it collides with
- Whether or not to collide with bodies in a specific group

When creating a `FixtureDef` object, there is a constructor that allows us to specify all the parameters:

```
    FixtureDef fixture = PhysicsFactory.createFixtureDef(density,
elasticity, friction, sensor, category, categoryMask, groupIndex);
```

Category is a number of the type `short`. This means that it is 16 bits long, and therefore, there are 16 categories. The other two parameters are of the type `short` as well.

Category

A fixture should belong to a single category only and will collide with every fixture in a category specified in category mask. A category has a number from 0 to 15. A fixture's category or categories are then specified by a single 16-bit number. A 16-bit number in the binary format consists of 16 zeroes and ones. We can index them from 0 to 15. If the fixture belongs to a category N, then the Nth bit will be 1. If it doesn't belong to the category, then the Nth bit will be 0.

A fixture can belong to multiple categories, but this only increases complexity.

There are 16 categories, but we will omit bits 5 to 16 and show just a simplified 4-bit example. We can imagine that there are 12 more zeroes prefixed to these numbers. Usually, the categories and masks are written as decimal numbers. The decimal number is simply the binary number with the base 10. We will see in the following example what this means:

Category	Binary	Decimal
0	0000	0
1	0001	1
2	0010	2
3	0100	4
4	1000	8

Now, if we want a fixture to belong to category 4, we will pass 8 to the constructor as its category.

The category mask

The category mask specifies with which other categories the fixture collides. It can collide with multiple categories. Specifying multiple categories using a single number can be done by adding the categories together. For example, if we want the fixture to collide with categories 1, 2, and 4, we will pass *1 + 2 + 8 = 11*. It might be easier to imagine it in the binary representation, as follows:

- 0001 +
- 0010 +
- 1000 =
- 1011

It is important that each number is on a new line.

1011_2 (base 2, binary) is 1110 (base 10, decimal). When two fixtures A and B collide, a simple check is calculated using a logical conjunction (the AND operator): *categoryA* AND *maskB* must not be 0 and at the same time *categoryB* AND *maskA* must not be 0. Here are the possible results of the AND operator:

- 0 AND 0 = 0
- 0 AND 1 = 0
- 1 AND 0 = 0
- 1 AND 1 = 1

So if a fixture is defined to collide with the category mask 1101 (=13), it will collide with any fixture that belongs to category 1, 3, or 4 (*1 + 4 + 8 = 13*). A few examples of collisions are as follows:

	A	B	C
Category mask	1100	1110	1111
Detected contact with category	0010	0010	0100
Result (AND)	0000	0010	0100
Collision happened?	No	Yes	Yes

For correct functionality of collisions, the masks and categories must be defined reflexively. Therefore, if a fixture belongs to category A and its mask defines that it collides with category B, fixtures in category B should define the mask that includes category A.

Example of categories and masks

The theory might be a bit difficult to grasp; let's see a real-world example in our game.

We are temporarily going to change the `populate()` method in GameScene to add our new objects. First, let's define some categories, as follows:

```
public static final short CATEGORY_BOX_1 = 1;
public static final short CATEGORY_BOX_2 = 2;
public static final short CATEGORY_CIRCLE = 4;
public static final short CATEGORY_PLATFORM = 8;
```

Then, we define masks, as follows:

```
public static final short MASK_ALL =
    CATEGORY_BOX_1 +
    CATEGORY_BOX_2 +
    CATEGORY_CIRCLE +
    CATEGORY_PLATFORM;

public static final short MASK_BOXES =
    CATEGORY_BOX_1 +
    CATEGORY_BOX_2 +
    CATEGORY_PLATFORM;

public static final short MASK_CIRCLE =
    CATEGORY_CIRCLE +
    CATEGORY_PLATFORM;
```

MASK_ALL means that the fixture collides with every other category. MASK_BOXES defines the fixture that collides with the platform and both boxes, and MASK_CIRCLE defines the fixture that collides with other circles and platforms.

Next, we temporarily stop the camera movement and remove the touch listener so that we can actually see a static scene with our new objects, as follows:

```
@Override
public void populate() {
  createBackground();
  createPlayer();
  //camera.setChaseEntity(player);
  createHUD();

  addPlatform(240, 100, false);
  addPlatform(340, 400, false);
  addEnemy(140, 400);

  engine.enableAccelerationSensor(activity, this);
  registerUpdateHandler(physicsWorld);

  //physicsWorld.setContactListener(new MyContactListener(player));


  ...

}
```

Finally, just after the commented line in the populate() method, we can add the new code, as follows:

```
FixtureDef boxFixture1 = PhysicsFactory.createFixtureDef(1f, 0f,
2f, false,
    CATEGORY_BOX_1, MASK_BOXES, (short) 0);
PhysicsFactory.createBoxBody(physicsWorld, 100, 300, 50, 25,
BodyType.DynamicBody, boxFixture1);
FixtureDef boxFixture2 = PhysicsFactory.createFixtureDef(1f, 0f,
2f, false,
    CATEGORY_BOX_2, MASK_BOXES, (short) 0);
PhysicsFactory.createBoxBody(physicsWorld, 130, 350, 50, 25,
BodyType.DynamicBody, boxFixture2);

FixtureDef circleFixture = PhysicsFactory.createFixtureDef(1f, 0f,
2f, false,
    CATEGORY_CIRCLE, MASK_CIRCLE, (short) 0);
Body circle = PhysicsFactory.createCircleBody(physicsWorld, 100,
440, 25, BodyType.DynamicBody, circleFixture);
```

```
        circle.setFixedRotation(true);

    FixtureDef platformFixture = PhysicsFactory.createFixtureDef(1f,
0f, 2f, false,
        CATEGORY_PLATFORM, MASK_ALL, (short) 0);
    PhysicsFactory.createBoxBody(physicsWorld, 100, 250, 150, 15,
BodyType.StaticBody, platformFixture);
```

This code defines four bodies; each of them belongs to a separate category. Right now, the circle and boxes don't collide, but the boxes collide with each other, as shown in the following screenshot:

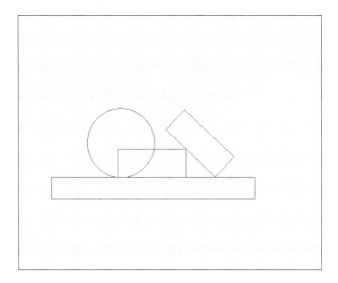

Thanks to the category definitions, we can very easily turn off collisions for the rectangles by removing the categories from MASK_BOXES, as follows:

```
    public static final short MASK_ALL =
        CATEGORY_BOX_1 +
        CATEGORY_BOX_2 +
        CATEGORY_CIRCLE +
        CATEGORY_PLATFORM;

    public static final short MASK_BOXES =
        CATEGORY_PLATFORM;

    public static final short MASK_CIRCLE =
        CATEGORY_CIRCLE +
        CATEGORY_PLATFORM;
```

The result looks as expected. The rectangular boxes now overlap too, as shown in the following screenshot:

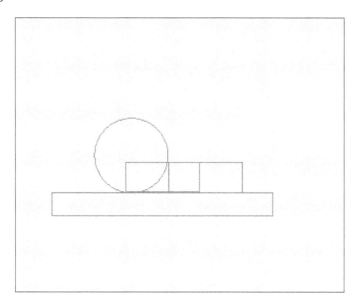

 The difference between collision filtering and sensors is that sensors don't influence their environment and other bodies but still detect collision and generate events for contact listener, whereas filtered collisions behave as if no collision happened at all.

Group index

The last parameter we can define when creating a fixture is group index. Group index is a positive or a negative number of a group. Members of the same group will either always collide with each other if the group number is positive, or never collide with each other if it is negative. Groups are different from categories and they have precedence over categories when deciding whether two objects collide or not.

In our example, if we defined both boxes and the circle in group 1, they would always collide. If we defined them with a negative group index, let's say -5, they would never collide. Group index 0 has no effect.

Here's an example how to make the boxes collide again without changing their categories or category masks. The change in the group index is highlighted in the following code:

```
    FixtureDef boxFixture1 = PhysicsFactory.createFixtureDef(1f, 0f,
2f, false,
        CATEGORY_BOX_1, MASK_BOXES, (short) 1);
    PhysicsFactory.createBoxBody(physicsWorld, 100, 300, 50, 20,
BodyType.DynamicBody, boxFixture1);
    FixtureDef boxFixture2 = PhysicsFactory.createFixtureDef(1f, 0f,
2f, false,
        CATEGORY_BOX_2, MASK_BOXES, (short) 1);
    PhysicsFactory.createBoxBody(physicsWorld, 130, 350, 50, 20,
BodyType.DynamicBody, boxFixture2);
```

Joints

When we need to connect two bodies together in Box2D, we use **joints**. Joints always connect two bodies and never more. Multiple joints are then required to link more bodies together. A joint always connects a dynamic body with another body that can be either static, kinematic, or dynamic. Joints between kinematic and static bodies are allowed but have no effect.

> Joints update the body positions and rotations based on the type of joint. You can define two bodies in an arbitrary location and rotation, but if the joint restricts the position, for example, the bodies will immediately transform to the proper position after the simulation starts.

A joint can also specify whether the connected bodies should collide or not. We are going to see the basic joints available in Box2D, and we are going to implement one of them.

The revolute joint

The revolute joint is like a pin or hinge. Imagine that you cut two bodies from some paper and pin them together. The pin hole in the first body is the first anchor and the hole in the second body is the second anchor. The bodies are linked with the pin and both can rotate around that point.

What's a bit hard to imagine is that the pin hole can actually be outside the bodies. We can think of this as if there was a small invisible solid unbendable wire with a little eye. Here's how a typical revolute joint looks:

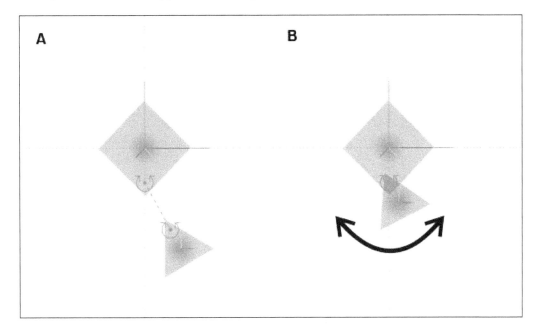

The joint is defined between a static square and a dynamic triangle. The circle arrows indicate where the joint anchors are. When we run the simulation, the triangle will be translated to the correct position and will then start rotating around the anchor.

A typical use for a revolute joint is a simple wheel on a cart, clock hands, or basically anything that revolves around a point.

The distance joint

The distance joint defines anchors in two bodies and a length. The two anchors will always keep the distance defined by the fixed length. We can imagine this joint as a steel rod mounted at the anchor positions between those two bodies. The bodies can rotate around the anchors unless they are defined with a fixed rotation. In the following figure, you can see two circles kept at the fixed distance.

The top circle rests on top of a static body. Without the joint, the lower circle will fall due to gravity.

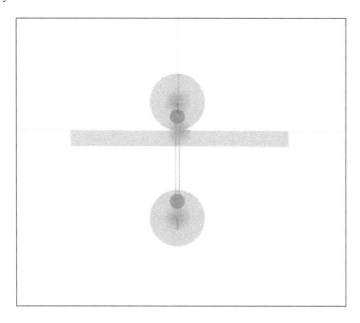

The prismatic joint

Two bodies linked with a prismatic joint will keep their relative rotation. If you rotate one, the other one will rotate too. However, they have one degree of freedom, they can move along a defined axis. We can imagine this as an elevator moving only up and down in the elevator shaft or a cylinder in a car's engine. The piston will move forward (up) and backwards (down) no matter how do you rotate the whole engine. Pistons and elevators are a typical use of this joint.

The prismatic joint can define a limit that will limit the movement (distance) of the bodies. In the following figure, the limit is shown and two thin green lines. The axis of movement is a green arrow. The upper body is static, so only the lower body moves. It can move as much as the limits permit.

The prismatic joint can also have a motor, which means that the bodies will try to move at a specified speed along the joint.

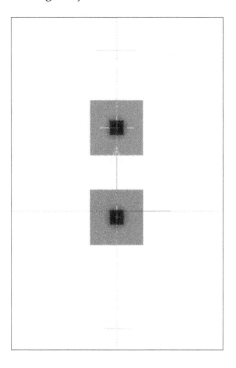

The line joint

The line joint is exactly the same as the prismatic joint, but the attached bodies can rotate. It is used to model vehicle suspensions.

The weld joint

The weld joint is very simple. It just holds two bodies together at a fixed position and rotation.

The friction joint

The friction joint adds friction between two bodies and thus reduces their relative speed. This joint is defined by the two bodies and a force. We can imagine it as a magnetic repulsive force between the two bodies.

The pulley joint

The pulley joint has two anchors, and the length from the first anchor to the first body summed with the length from the second anchor to the second body is always the same. Here's a typical example of how it works:

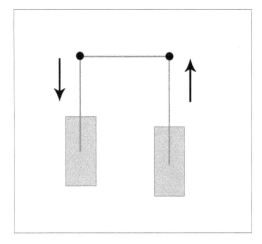

The behavior can be changed by a constant that will make one of the ropes extend and contract constant times faster than the other side.

The gear joint

The gear joint is the only joint that connects two other joints. We still have to define two bodies but we must also pass two joints to the gear joint. Let's say we have one static body called Ground and two dynamic smaller bodies, A and B, attached to the ground using a revolute joint. When we define a gear joint between A and B, we also have to pass the joints' Ground-A and Ground-B joint definitions to the gear joint. Then, the Ground-A joint makes A move, and B will move as well. The revolute and prismatic joints can be linked with a gear joint.

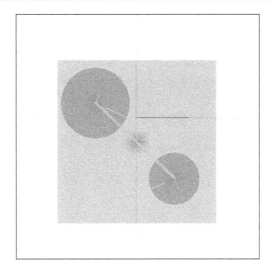

The mouse joint

The last joint is called the mouse joint and it is special because it only requires one body, but still two bodies must be passed in. One of the bodies is the body that we want to move and the other one can be any body.

A mouse joint is used to move a body to another location. Basically we define a point (anchor) on a body and a target. It will look as if we have attached a string at the anchor and pulled the string towards us while standing at the target location. The properties of the string can also be defined. For example, we can make the string to elastic and the body will bounce around the target before settling in.

A typical use for the mouse joint is a go-to feature or the drag-and-drop feature in physics-based games.

Implementing a revolute joint

The good thing about joints is that most of them can be defined the same way, just some parameters and the final effect differ. Here's a simple way to attach one of the temporarily added bodies to the player's body. The code belongs to the `populate()` method of the `GameScene` class. We have removed the temporary bodies except the circle and we no longer need filtering:

```
@Override
public void populate() {
  createBackground();
  createPlayer();
```

```
    //camera.setChaseEntity(player);
    createHUD();

    addPlatform(240, 100, false);
    addPlatform(340, 400, false);
    addEnemy(140, 400);

    engine.enableAccelerationSensor(activity, this);
    registerUpdateHandler(physicsWorld);

    //physicsWorld.setContactListener(new MyContactListener(player));

    setOnSceneTouchListener(this);

    FixtureDef circleFixture = PhysicsFactory.createFixtureDef(1f, 0f,
2f, false);
    Body circle = PhysicsFactory.createCircleBody(physicsWorld, 80,
440, 25, BodyType.DynamicBody, circleFixture);
    circle.setFixedRotation(false);

    RevoluteJointDef revoluteJointDef = new RevoluteJointDef();
    revoluteJointDef.bodyA = player.getBody();
    revoluteJointDef.bodyB = circle;
    revoluteJointDef.localAnchorA.set(new Vector2(-1, 0));
    revoluteJointDef.localAnchorB.set(new Vector2(0, 0.6f));
    revoluteJointDef.collideConnected = false;
    physicsWorld.createJoint(revoluteJointDef);

    DebugRenderer dr = new DebugRenderer(physicsWorld, vbom);
    dr.setZIndex(999);
    attachChild(dr);
}
```

The highlighted code sets the rotation of the circle to false. Without this, the revolute joint would be just a weld joint in the end. To create a joint, we start by creating the appropriate definition, in this case, the RevoluteJointDef object. We set both bodies and then set the local anchors. The anchor A defines the point of attachment one meter to the left from the player's center. The anchor point B defines the point of attachment in the top part of the circle, 0.6 meters up from the center. We also turn off the collisions between the bodies. Finally, we call the physicsWorld method to create the joint.

When we run the game now, the character will have a small circle attached to its head that swings freely around the point of attachment. The effect is visible because there isn't any sprite attached to the circle, only thanks to the debug renderer.

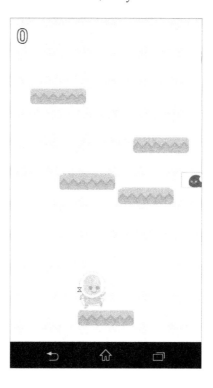

We can also configure a motor in the joint that will make the circle rotate automatically. The player's character will not rotate because it is configured with a fixed rotation set to true, as follows:

```
revoluteJointDef.motorSpeed = 100f;
revoluteJointDef.maxMotorTorque = 20f;
revoluteJointDef.enableMotor = true;
```

The motor speed is the target speed, and the torque is a rotational force that it can use to get to the target speed. Setting this as low will make the motor reach the final speed very slowly and vice versa.

Summary

In this chapter, we learned three advanced concepts in the physics engine. First, we talked about assembling bodies from multiple fixtures that can produce better fitting bodies. We have also seen how to use different types of fixtures in a single body to produce interesting effects. Secondly, we have learned what collision filtering is and how to use it to specify which bodies should collide and which should not. Finally, a brief introduction to joints was given and one of the joints was implemented.

In the next chapter, we are going back to our game and will add additional scenes: the splash, the menu, and the loading scene. We are going to see how to load resources in the background and show a message or an image in the meantime. We will also learn how to create persistent data in the game.

9
Adding a Menu and Splash Scene

A splash scene is very important, not only because it shows your logo or any other logos you want to show, but it also gives the players something to look at while loading the resources in the background.

A menu scene serves as the entry point to the game. Even if your game is really simple, there should be a screen that at least says *Tap to Start*. It can actually be the game scene, paused and displaying the text. Nevertheless, it should be there.

In this chapter, we are going to add a splash and menu scene to our game. We will also learn how to load the resources in the background. We are going to create a loading scene as well as a transition from the menu to the game scene and back. We will also add an option to enable and disable sound that will be available from our menu scene.

While it may sound counterintuitive to add the scenes that the user sees at the start of the game only now after we have almost finished the game, it's actually the preferred way. First, we have created the gameplay and seen that our idea is viable. Second, thanks to having no extra screens, every time we ran the game, we went straight to the game. Finally, we have kept the code organized in a way that makes it easy to add the additional scenes.

Managing multiple scenes

We need another manager class that will take care of switching the scenes. However, the code depends on the other scenes and, therefore, we are going to create the classes for the scenes first.

A splash scene

A typical splash scene shows a logo of the game maker. Sometimes, it also shows copyrights and can be split into multiple screens when there is a need to show multiple logos — typically the game author, the publisher, and sometimes the engine logo.

We are going to use the AndEngine logo. It is included in the source code of this chapter.

Updating the resource manager

Because we are using another resource, we need to update our `ResourceManager` class. This time, we are going to create a method for both loading and unloading the splash image.

 In games that require a lot of resources, the graphics that are no longer used should be unloaded to prevent out of memory errors.

The following is the new code that we need to add:

```
// splash graphics
public ITextureRegion splashTextureRegion;
private BitmapTextureAtlas splashTextureAtlas;
public void loadSplashGraphics() {
  BitmapTextureAtlasTextureRegionFactory.setAssetBasePath("gfx/");
  splashTextureAtlas = new
    BitmapTextureAtlas(activity.getTextureManager(), 256, 256,
    BitmapTextureFormat.RGBA_8888,
    TextureOptions.BILINEAR_PREMULTIPLYALPHA);

  splashTextureRegion = BitmapTextureAtlasTextureRegionFactory.
    createFromAsset(splashTextureAtlas, activity.getAssets(),
    "badge.png", 0, 0);
```

```
   splashTextureAtlas.load();
  }

  public void unloadSplashGraphics() {
    splashTextureAtlas.unload();
  }
```

We are declaring a new atlas and a texture region. We do not need to use a buildable type of atlas because we are loading only a single image. That's why we are passing the extra integer parameters in the following call:

```
  splashTextureRegion = BitmapTextureAtlasTextureRegionFactory.
    createFromAsset(splashTextureAtlas, activity.getAssets(),
    "badge.png", 0, 0);
```

We are adding the image to the atlas at the position (0, 0). The `unload` method unloads everything from this atlas, which is just the logo in our case.

Creating the scene

All scene classes belong to the `is.kul.learningandengine.scene` package. Let's create a new scene class called simply `SplashScene` and let it extend the `AbstractScene` class:

```
  public class SplashScene extends AbstractScene {

    @Override
    public void populate() {
      Sprite splashSprite = new Sprite(GameActivity.CAMERA_WIDTH /
        2, GameActivity.CAMERA_HEIGHT / 2, res.splashTextureRegion,
        vbom);
      attachChild(splashSprite);
    }

    @Override
    public void onPause() {
    }

    @Override
    public void onResume() {
    }
  }
```

The scene is very simple. There's just a single sprite in the middle of the screen showing the logo of AndEngine. The following screenshot shows what the scene looks like:

Loading of the resources is not done in the scene itself. We are going to add the code that loads them later, when we put all the scenes together.

The menu scene

AndEngine has a class that is called MenuScene, and this class can be used for our purposes. Of course, we can create our own class and add all the functionality ourselves. We can use sprites and their touch areas. But to create a simple menu scene fast, we are going to use the AndEngine functionality.

The MenuScene class is a camera scene, which means it will move along with the camera. In our case, it doesn't matter because our menu scene will be still. It allows us to add menu items that can have simple animations and a number that identifies the item. There's also a listener that handles the taps on the menu items.

To fit the menu scene to our system of classes, we are going to create a MenuSceneWrapper class first. We are going to add only a single item to the menu for now. This can be done as follows:

```
public class MenuSceneWrapper extends AbstractScene implements
    IOnMenuItemClickListener {
```

```
private IMenuItem playMenuItem;

@Override
public void populate() {

  MenuScene menuScene = new MenuScene(camera);
  menuScene.getBackground().setColor(0.82f, 0.96f, 0.97f);

  playMenuItem = new ColorMenuItemDecorator(new TextMenuItem(0,
    res.font, "PLAY", vbom), Color.CYAN, Color.WHITE);

  menuScene.addMenuItem(playMenuItem);

  menuScene.buildAnimations();
  menuScene.setBackgroundEnabled(true);

  menuScene.setOnMenuItemClickListener(this);

  Sprite player = new Sprite(240, 280, res.playerTextureRegion,
    vbom);
  menuScene.attachChild(player);

  setChildScene(menuScene);

}

@Override
public void onPause() {
}

@Override
public void onResume() {
}

@Override
public boolean onMenuItemClicked(MenuScene pMenuScene, IMenuItem
  pMenuItem, float pMenuItemLocalX, float pMenuItemLocalY) {
  switch (pMenuItem.getID()) {
    case 0 :
    // show the game scene here
    return true;
    default :
```

```
        return false;
      }
   }

   @Override
   public void onBackKeyPressed() {
     activity.finish();
   }

}
```

In the `populate()` method, we first create the `MenuScene` class. Then, we create a `TextMenuItem` object. There are two options in AndEngine, the second being a `SpriteMenuItem` object. While the former can only show text using the fonts we have loaded before, the latter can show an arbitrary image.

We are wrapping the `TextMenuItem` into a `ColorMenuItemDecorator`, which is a class that can change the color of the text on touch. Two color values are passed: the default and the touched text color. The other implemented decorator class in AndEngine is the `ScaleMenuItemDecorator` class that can scale the item on touch.

The `buildAnimations()` method will position the menu items automatically and prepare the animations defined by the decorators. The `setBackgroundEnabled()` method is used to either enable or disable the background of the camera scene. Usually, this is set to `false` so that the underlying scene is shown, but we have set the color of the menu background and we want to see it, so therefore we are passing `true`.

As a little decoration, we also add our player image under the menu items.

We also set our wrapper class to be the listener for touches. For this to work, our class must implement the `IOnMenuItemClickListener` method, which declares a method called `onMenuItemClicked()`. In this method, we decide what action to take on a touched menu item based on its numerical identifier. In our case, this is showing the game scene in case the menu item with identifier 0 was touched. We do not have any other menu items yet.

Finally, we return `true` if we consider the touch handled or `false` if it was not handled.

The last method, `onBackKeyPressed()`, tells the app to finish the activity, effectively closing the game, when the user presses the back key in the menu.

To exit a Java program, you can usually use `System.exit(errorCode);`. But in an Android environment, this is not safe because the system might have open handles, for example, a cache that was not saved or cleared. Using `activity.finish()` is recommended, because it will properly release all the resources.

The following screenshot shows a preview of the menu scene:

The loading scene

A loading scene is very simple and is used in a similar way as a theater curtain. The typical use is to show the loading screen when another scene is requested. Then, tear down the old scene, load new resources, and build the new scene, and finally hide the loading scene and show the new scene.

Here's the code:

```
public class LoadingScene extends AbstractScene {

    @Override
    public void populate() {
```

```java
    CameraScene cameraScene = new CameraScene(camera);

    Text text = new Text(GameActivity.CAMERA_WIDTH / 2,
      GameActivity.CAMERA_HEIGHT / 2, res.font, "LOADING...",
      vbom);
    cameraScene.attachChild(text);

    setChildScene(cameraScene);
  }

  @Override
  public void onPause() {
  }

  @Override
  public void onResume() {
  }

}
```

This is one of the simplest loading screens possible. It just prints **LOADING...** in the middle of the screen. This is shown in the following screenshot:

The scene manager

Now that we have the required scenes, we have to create a mechanism to change from one to the other. We want a class that will be accessible from everywhere in the game. We are going to use the same pattern we have used for our `ResourceManager` class and create a singleton `SceneManager` class. The code is a bit long, so let's write it piece by piece. To begin, we create an empty class in the `is.kul.learningandengine` package and make it a singleton. The code is as follows:

```
public class SceneManager {

    // single instance is created only
    private static final SceneManager INSTANCE = new SceneManager();
    public static final long SPLASH_DURATION = 2000;

    private ResourceManager res = ResourceManager.getInstance();

    private AbstractScene currentScene;

    private LoadingScene loadingScene = null;

    private SceneManager() { }

    public static SceneManager getInstance() {
        return INSTANCE;
    }

    public AbstractScene getCurrentScene() {
        return currentScene;
    }

    public void setCurrentScene(AbstractScene currentScene) {
        this.currentScene = currentScene;
        res.engine.setScene(currentScene);
        Debug.i("Current scene: " + currentScene.getClass().
            getName());
    }
}
```

We have already added some fields and constants. We are going to need a handle to the current scene, and also, we want to create the loading scene only once and keep it, so it will be easy to show it when necessary. The `SPLASH_DURATION` constant is a minimum time in milliseconds for which the splash will be shown. Finally, there is a setter and a getter for the `currentScene` class. The setter switches the current scene in the engine as well and logs the current scene class name to LogCat.

The next method, called showSplashAndMenuScene(), will be called at the beginning of the game. It is as follows:

```
public AbstractScene showSplashAndMenuScene() {
  final SplashScene splashScene = new SplashScene();
  splashScene.populate();
  setCurrentScene(splashScene);

  new AsyncTask<Void, Void, Void>() {
    @Override
    protected Void doInBackground(Void... params) {
      long timestamp = System.currentTimeMillis();
      res.loadFont();
      res.loadGameAudio();
      res.loadGameGraphics();

      loadingScene = new LoadingScene();
      loadingScene.populate();

      AbstractScene nextScene = new MenuSceneWrapper();

      if (System.currentTimeMillis() - timestamp <
        SPLASH_DURATION) {
        try {
          Thread.sleep(SPLASH_DURATION -
            (System.currentTimeMillis() - timestamp) );
        } catch (InterruptedException e) {
          Debug.e("Interrupted", e);
        }
      }
      nextScene.populate();
      setCurrentScene(nextScene);
      splashScene.destroy();
      res.unloadSplashGraphics();
      return null;
    }
  }.execute();
  return splashScene;
}
```

This method creates an extra thread, and it works by first creating and populating the splash scene. The splash scene resources must be already loaded at this time. We have to update the GameActivity class due to this fact. Then, create and execute a **background task**.

A background task is Android's way of running something in a background thread. It is a very useful mechanism that has a lot of uses, but it can get a little bit complicated. For now, we will stick to the simplest use case. We will only run a piece of code in the background.

 The other uses are, for example, showing a status bar. The background task can define a value that will serve as the progress value.

The code inside the background task first creates a timestamp. Then, it loads all resources and prepares the loading screen. If this does not take the time defined as SPLASH_DURATION, then it waits until the time is up.

Then, it populates the next scene and sets it as the current scene. At this point, the scene starts showing. Finally, it unloads the resources and destroys the splash scene. The destroy() method is just our method that we can use to do some clean up if necessary.

Now, we add two methods that switch the menu scene to the game scene and vice versa. The first method is as follows:

```
public void showGameScene() {
    final AbstractScene previousScene = getCurrentScene();
    setCurrentScene(loadingScene);
    new AsyncTask<Void, Void, Void>() {

        @Override
        protected Void doInBackground(Void... params) {
            GameScene gameScene = new GameScene();
            gameScene.populate();
            setCurrentScene(gameScene);
            previousScene.destroy();

            return null;
        }
    }.execute();
}
```

This method uses the background task as well. It shows the loading scene first, and then executes the task. The task itself creates the new scene, shows the new scene, and finally destroys the previous scene.

The other method looks exactly the same, just with the classes swapped:

```
public void showMenuScene() {
  final AbstractScene previousScene = getCurrentScene();
  setCurrentScene(loadingScene);
  new AsyncTask<Void, Void, Void>() {

    @Override
    protected Void doInBackground(Void... params) {
      MenuSceneWrapper menuSceneWrapper = new MenuSceneWrapper();
      menuSceneWrapper.populate();
      setCurrentScene(menuSceneWrapper);
      previousScene.destroy();
      return null;
    }
  }.execute();
}
```

That's it, we have our `SceneManager` class which is ready to use.

Plugging in the SceneManager class

Finally, we have to update other classes to make our `SceneManager` class work properly. Let's first start with the `GameScene` class.

On back key press, we want the game to go back to the menu. Let's change the `GameScene` class and override the relevant method:

```
@Override
public void onBackKeyPressed() {
  SceneManager.getInstance().showMenuScene();
}
```

The rest of the changes must be done in the `GameActivity` class. Three methods have to be changed and one added:

```
@Override
public void onCreateResources(
  OnCreateResourcesCallback pOnCreateResourcesCallback)
  throws IOException {
  ResourceManager.getInstance().create(this, getEngine(),
    getEngine().getCamera(), getVertexBufferObjectManager());
  ResourceManager.getInstance().loadSplashGraphics();
  pOnCreateResourcesCallback.onCreateResourcesFinished();
}
```

In the `onCreateResources()` method, we no longer load all of the resources, but only those needed for the splash scene. Now, consider the following code:

```
@Override
public void onCreateScene(OnCreateSceneCallback
  pOnCreateSceneCallback)
  throws IOException {
  // we just have to pass something to the callback
  pOnCreateSceneCallback.onCreateSceneFinished(null);
}
```

We are now effectively ignoring the `onCreateScene()` method, because we have only one method to call in the `SceneManager` class. We are going to call it in the next method:

```
@Override
public void onPopulateScene(Scene pScene, OnPopulateSceneCallback
  pOnPopulateSceneCallback)
  throws IOException {
  SceneManager.getInstance().showSplashAndMenuScene();
  pOnPopulateSceneCallback.onPopulateSceneFinished();
}
```

Finally, we add a method that checks the key press event and calls the appropriate method from the current scene:

```
@Override
public boolean onKeyDown(int keyCode, KeyEvent event) {
  if (keyCode == KeyEvent.KEYCODE_BACK) {
    SceneManager.getInstance().getCurrentScene().
      onBackKeyPressed();
    return true;
  }
  return super.onKeyDown(keyCode, event);
}
```

This method will exit the game in the menu scene and return to the menu scene from the game scene. It will ignore the back key in the splash and loading scene, because those two scenes do not override the `onBackKeyPressed()` method. The method returns `true` to indicate that the back key press was handled.

 The usual behavior is to return to the previous activity. Since we have only one activity, the Android system would return to the activity that started the game, probably the launcher.

That's all. When we run the game now, it will start with a splash screen, show it for two seconds, and then show our simple menu scene. When we tap on the **PLAY** text, the loading screen will show for just a fraction of a second and the game will start. To return to the menu, we can press the back key.

We can use a simple trick to show the loading screen for a little bit longer. The following code shows a change to the showGameScene() method:

```
public void showGameScene() {
    final AbstractScene previousScene = getCurrentScene();
    setCurrentScene(loadingScene);
    new AsyncTask<Void, Void, Void>() {

        @Override
        protected Void doInBackground(Void... params) {
            try {
                Thread.sleep(1000);
            } catch (InterruptedException e) {
                Debug.e("Interrupted", e);
            }
            GameScene gameScene = new GameScene();
            gameScene.populate();
            previousScene.destroy();

            setCurrentScene(gameScene);
            return null;
        }

    }.execute();

}
```

Now, the loading screen will be displayed for at least a second.

Storing values

From time to time, we need to persist some values. Typical examples are a high score or the settings of our game. AndEngine doesn't have any built-in mechanism for this, but we can use the Android SDK to achieve it.

There are two ways. A simple way is to use **shared preferences**, which is a key-value persistent storage. A more robust but more complicated way is to use the SQLite database, which is accessible from every Android application. We are going to use the simple way to store the high score and sound settings.

Using preferences

Each application has access to its `Preferences` object. It's basically a key-value map. It is very simple to use preferences, but it's easy to make a mistake. First, we need to initialize the storage. This is done with the following code:

```
SharedPreferences settings = getSharedPreferences
  ("andengine_game_prefs", MODE_PRIVATE);
```

We can have multiple preferences and they are identified by the name. This is the first parameter and any name will do. The second parameter is a mode of access. There are four modes of access, as follows:

- `MODE_PRIVATE`: This is shared only in your application.
- `MODE_WORLD_READABLE`: In this, all the other applications can read the shared preferences if they know the name. This can cause security issues.
- `MODE_WORLD_WRITEABLE`: In this, other applications can even write to the shared preferences. This can cause big security issues.
- `MODE_MULTI_PROCESS`: This was used before for multiprocess access.

To retrieve the value, a simple call is used:

```
settings.getInt(key, defaultValue);
```

There are methods to retrieve all basic types, not just an integer. The key is a string key, which is the name of the preference. In case the value doesn't exist in the storage, the `defaultValue` is returned instead.

Saving a value needs a little bit more code, as follows:

```
SharedPreferences.Editor settingsEditor = settings.edit();
settingsEditor.putInt(key, value);
settingsEditor.commit();
```

The `commit()` method ensures that the values are persisted. The following is the complete code we need to add to the `GameActivity` class:

```
private final String KEY_SOUND = "Sound";
private final String KEY_HISCORE = "HiScore";

SharedPreferences settings;

public void setSound(boolean sound) {
  SharedPreferences.Editor settingsEditor = settings.edit();
  settingsEditor.putBoolean(KEY_SOUND, sound);
```

```
    settingsEditor.commit();
  }

  public boolean isSound() {
    return settings.getBoolean(KEY_SOUND, true);
  }

  public void setHiScore(int score) {
    SharedPreferences.Editor settingsEditor = settings.edit();
    settingsEditor.putInt(KEY_HISCORE, score);
    settingsEditor.commit();
  }

  public int getHiScore() {
    return settings.getInt(KEY_HISCORE, 0);
  }

  @Override
  public EngineOptions onCreateEngineOptions() {
    settings = getSharedPreferences("andengine_game_prefs",
      MODE_PRIVATE);
    ...
  }
```

There are two values we want to store. We define the keys as constants and create the setters and getters. We are initializing the preferences in the first method that gets called by AndEngine.

Settings

Now that we can save the value of sound (on or off), we would like to give the user the option to change the settings. We can add another menu item to the menu scene. We also want to indicate whether the sound is currently on or off. Unfortunately, the default menu items in AndEngine don't allow us to change the text. But, we can of course create our own menu item. The following is a custom text menu item decorator that allows us to change the text. We can put it in the same package as the MenuSceneWrapper class.

```
  public class MyTextMenuItemDecorator extends
    ColorMenuItemDecorator {

    private TextMenuItem textMenuItem;

    public MyTextMenuItemDecorator(TextMenuItem textMenuItem, Color
      pSelectedColor, Color pUnselectedColor) {
      super(textMenuItem, pSelectedColor, pUnselectedColor);
```

```
    this.textMenuItem = textMenuItem;
  }

  public void setText(CharSequence text) {
    textMenuItem.setText(text);
  }

}
```

It is basically the same as the `ColorMenuItemDecorator` class, but it has a handle to `textMenuItem`, and this allows us to change the text. Now, we can change the `MenuSceneWrapper` class. The changes are highlighted in the following code:

```
public class MenuSceneWrapper extends AbstractScene implements
  IOnMenuItemClickListener {

  private IMenuItem playMenuItem;
  private MyTextMenuItemDecorator soundMenuItem;

  @Override
  public void populate() {

    MenuScene menuScene = new MenuScene(camera);
    menuScene.getBackground().setColor(0.82f, 0.96f, 0.97f);

    playMenuItem = new ColorMenuItemDecorator(new TextMenuItem(0,
      res.font, "PLAY", vbom), Color.CYAN, Color.WHITE);

    soundMenuItem = new MyTextMenuItemDecorator(new TextMenuItem
      (1, res.font, getSoundLabel(), vbom), Color.CYAN,
      Color.WHITE);

    menuScene.addMenuItem(playMenuItem);
    menuScene.addMenuItem(soundMenuItem);

    menuScene.buildAnimations();
    menuScene.setBackgroundEnabled(true);

    menuScene.setOnMenuItemClickListener(this);

    Sprite player = new Sprite(240, 280, res.playerTextureRegion,
      vbom);
    menuScene.attachChild(player);

    setChildScene(menuScene);

  }

  private CharSequence getSoundLabel() {
    return activity.isSound() ? "SOUND ON" : "SOUND OFF";
  }
```

```
@Override
public boolean onMenuItemClicked(MenuScene pMenuScene, IMenuItem
  pMenuItem, float pMenuItemLocalX, float pMenuItemLocalY) {
  switch (pMenuItem.getID()) {
    case 0 :
      SceneManager.getInstance().showGameScene();
      return true;
    case 1 :
      boolean soundState = activity.isSound();
      soundState = !soundState;
      activity.setSound(soundState);
      soundMenuItem.setText(getSoundLabel());
      return true;
    default :
      return false;
  }
}
}
```

We create this menu item the same way as we did the previous one. When the option in the menu is touched, the state of the sound setting is changed from true to false or false to true, and then the value is stored in the preferences again.

The menu screen should now look like the following screenshot:

Playing sound according to the settings

Another thing we need is to play the sound only when the sound is enabled. We need to centralize the way we play sounds, because right now we simply call the `sound.play()` method, and it would be impossible to control it this way.

Let's add one last method to the `GameActivity` class:

```
public void playSound(Sound soundToPlay) {
  if (isSound()) {
    soundToPlay.play();
  }
}
```

This method checks whether the sound is currently enabled and only then plays the sound. The following code shows how we can use it in the `Player` class:

```
public void die() {
  if (!dead) {
    ResourceManager.getInstance().activity.playSound(
      ResourceManager.getInstance().soundFall);
  }
  setDead(true);
  setCurrentTileIndex(2);
}
```

It can also be used in the `MyContactListener` class as follows:

```
@Override
public void preSolve(Contact contact, Manifold oldManifold) {
  if (checkContact(contact, Player.TYPE, Platform.TYPE)) {
    // player and platform
    if (!player.isDead() && player.getBody().getLinearVelocity().y
      < 0) {
      player.getBody().setLinearVelocity(new Vector2(0, 40));
      ResourceManager.getInstance().activity.playSound(
        ResourceManager.getInstance().soundJump);
    } else {
      contact.setEnabled(false);
    }
  }
}
```

High score

As the last thing in this chapter, we will add a persistent high score to our game. We can already save and retrieve it, but now we need to save it at the right time and display it somewhere.

We are checking for the game over event in the onManagedUpdate() method of the GameScene class. We will save the score there in case the score surpassed the last high score. This can be done as follows:

```
if (player.isDead()) {
  endGameText.setVisible(true);
  if (score > activity.getHiScore()) {
    activity.setHiScore(score);
  }
}
```

To display it, we can add it as text to the menu scene. The following is the code change necessary in the populate() method of the MenuSceneWrapper class:

```
@Override
public void populate() {

    ...

    Sprite player = new Sprite(240, 280, res.playerTextureRegion,
        vbom);
    menuScene.attachChild(player);

    Text hiscoreText = new Text(240, 600, res.font, "HISCORE: " +
        activity.getHiScore(), vbom);
    menuScene.attachChild(hiscoreText);

    setChildScene(menuScene);

}
```

The following screenshot shows what the final version of the menu scene looks like:

Summary

In this chapter, we learned how to work with multiple scenes. We have added a splash scene to show a logo, a menu scene that can alter the game settings and show the high score, and a loading scene to make the transition from one scene to another. We now also know how to load resources in the background and how to unload the unnecessary resources to free the memory.

Our game is now complete. It's not particularly pretty and the gameplay rules need a lot of tuning, but it works and it has all the essential features a simple game like this needs.

In the next chapter, we will look into polishing our game a little bit more. We will add music and a few special effects. We are going to use more animations, particle systems, and parallax background to add a 3D feeling to the game. Finally, we will learn a little bit about shaders—what they are and how they can make our game look better.

10
Polishing the Game

We've made it all the way here to chapter 10 where we will polish our game. We already have a game, it plays, and it has all the necessities of a mobile game. However, we can still make it much better and make it look more professional. We can add eye candy, music, and fine-tune the rules. In this chapter, we will introduce several things that can improve the overall look and feel of the game.

We will add music to our game in this chapter and we are going to learn more about entity modifiers and how they can improve our game by adding animations. We will also understand what a particle system is and learn how to use it. To add a simple 3D effect, we are going to utilize a parallax background. And at the end of this chapter, we will see what shaders are and how are they used in modern games.

What is polishing?

Polishing is what a game needs; however, nobody can exactly define what it means. If we try to simplify it, polishing means making the game better. It can mean adding better music and sound effects, adding visual effects, and making the game play more interesting and the game more stable and optimized. We will not polish our game completely, because we won't discuss polishing the game play itself. That is a topic for another book. However, we will discuss where we can polish our game with respect to audiovisuals and learn how to achieve it.

Adding music

Music is different from sounds in Android. While sound files are usually short and they are loaded into the memory, music files tend to be quite large and they are streamed from the storage and only a part of the music file is currently in memory. Also, only one music file can play at a single time.

The other problem with music files being quite large is that they take up valuable space. The APK archive is limited to 50 MB. While simple games tend to be much smaller, in resource-rich games the limit can be reached quite easily.

> Up to two expansion files, 2 GB each, can be added to the game. You can learn more about expansion files at http://developer. android.com/google/play/expansion-files.html.

We have already loaded the music file in our game and now we only have to play it. Let's limit the music to the game scene only. However, first, we will write a small convenience class for playing music that will take into account our sound settings. We will call it `MusicPlayer` and it belongs to the `is.kul.learningandengine` package. The code is as follows:

```
public class MusicPlayer {

    private static MusicPlayer INSTANCE = new MusicPlayer();

    private ResourceManager res;

    private MusicPlayer() {
        res = ResourceManager.getInstance();
    }

    public static MusicPlayer getInstance() {
        return INSTANCE;
    }

    public void play() {
        if (res.activity.isSound() && !res.music.isPlaying()) {
            res.music.play();
        }
    }

    public void pause() {
        if (res.music.isPlaying()) {
            res.music.pause();
        }
    }

    public void stop() {
        if (res.music.isPlaying()) {
            res.music.pause();
            res.music.seekTo(0);
        }
    }
}
```

We will follow the singleton pattern and there are three new methods: `play()`, `pause()`, and `stop()`. They do exactly what the names suggest. The first method, `play()`, checks whether the sound is enabled and the music is not playing and if both conditions are true, it starts the music. The default behavior of this method is infinite looping. Volume can also be adjusted, but we will simply play it on the default volume. The `pause()` method just checks whether the music is playing. The last method called `stop()` actually doesn't stop the music, but it pauses it and rewinds the track. The reason for this little workaround is that AndEngine wraps the `MediaPlayer` class that represents the Android *media player* in another class called `Music`, which doesn't offer all methods and doesn't handle the music perfectly.

Life cycle of the media player

The media player has a quite complicated life cycle. AndEngine tries to hide it from game developers and tries to simplify it. Here's the complete life cycle of the media player:

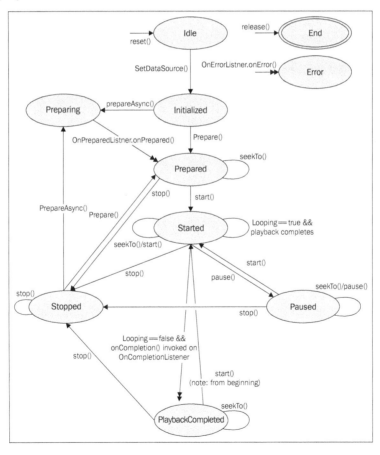

The problematic part is when the media is stopped. It gets released and AndEngine doesn't offer the `prepare()` method; therefore, we will have to use the `getMediaPlayer()` method and then use the `prepare()` method directly. Because the media track must be rewound after `prepare()` anyway, we can use a little trick. We will never let the music stop and only pause it and rewind it if necessary. This way we can avoid the problem altogether.

> The most common error when working with a media player is **X called in state N**, where N is an integer number and X is the state we wanted. This error is always caused by trying to advance to an invalid state from the current one.

Using the new manager class is very easy, but we have to use it as the right moment. Starting the music in the `populate()` method of the `GameScene` class is a good idea, as shown in the following code:

```
@Override
public void populate() {
    createBackground();
    createPlayer();
    camera.setChaseEntity(player);
    createHUD();

    addPlatform(240, 100, false);
    addPlatform(340, 400, false);
    addEnemy(140, 400);

    engine.enableAccelerationSensor(activity, this);
    registerUpdateHandler(physicsWorld);

    physicsWorld.setContactListener(new MyContactListener(player));

    setOnSceneTouchListener(this);
    MusicPlayer.getInstance().play();
}
```

This will work nicely; it will start the music just after the whole scene is populated. However, when the user goes back to the menu, the music will be still playing because the media player and therefore the `Music` class plays the music in the background and is not tied to the scene in any way. To stop playing the music when we go back, we can stop it in the `destroy()` method of the `GameScene` class, as follows:

```
@Override
public void destroy() {
```

```
      camera.reset();
      camera.setHUD(null);
      MusicPlayer.getInstance().stop();
  }
```

However, that is still not enough. What happens when the user presses the Home button or receives an incoming call? Well, the answer is the music will be still playing. We need to stop the music when the game is automatically paused and sent to background and play it again when it is resumed. AndEngine gives us two convenient hooks for this purpose in the `BaseGameActivity` class. Let's make use of them. We are going to override them in our `GameActivity` class and add our own behavior based on the current scene, as follows:

```
  @Override
  public synchronized void onResumeGame() {
    super.onResumeGame();
    SceneManager.getInstance().getCurrentScene().onResume();
  }

  @Override
  public synchronized void onPauseGame() {
    super.onPauseGame();
    SceneManager.getInstance().getCurrentScene().onPause();
  }
```

We have defined the `onResume()` and `onPause()` methods in `AbstractScene`. This is how we can now utilize them in the `GameScene` class:

```
  @Override
  public void onPause() {
    MusicPlayer.getInstance().pause();
  }

  @Override
  public void onResume() {
    MusicPlayer.getInstance().play();
  }
```

And that's it. The music will stop in `onPause()` and start playing in `onResume()`.

> We have defined these methods as abstract with no default behavior in the `AbstractScene` class. This means, that all scenes must define some behavior. This is a good way to make sure everything that needs to be stopped when the game is interrupted is stopped and resumed when the user returns to the game.

Adding animations using entity modifiers

We used animations in *Chapter 5*, *Basic Interactions*, and in *Chapter 6*, *Physics*, we learned how to use the physics engine to move objects. We are going to use the same techniques from *Chapter 5*, *Basic Interactions*, to create simple animated effects and we will use them in the menu scene. We are going to cover entity modifiers in more detail here.

As we already learned, entity modifiers are used for tweening: changing a position, rotation, or size of an object from one state to another. We also know that the tweening can be linear, which means the same speed of change from state A to state B for the whole duration, or we can use easing functions to change the behavior of the tween.

Chaining modifiers

The entity modifiers can also be chained together. A sprite can rotate and move at the same time. There are two ways of chaining: parallel and sequence.

The following figure shows how parallel chaining looks. All the modifiers will run at the same time, but they might not finish at the same time. Each modifier also defines two callback hooks at the beginning and at the end of a modifier and we perform any action at that moment:

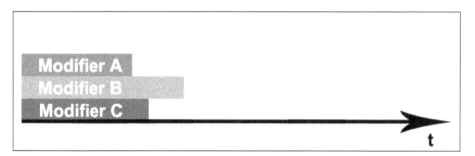

The sequence modifier works as expected. Each modifier is run after the previous has finished. Again, the callback hooks can be used. Have a look at the following figure:

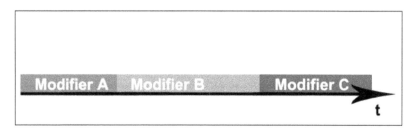

There's also a loop entity modifier that makes any modifier or chain of modifiers loop either indefinitely or a specified number of times. This can be used to indefinitely rotate an object.

Here's a code example of chaining. Both sequence and parallel modifiers can be nested indefinitely or until we run out of memory or processing power. The following code is from `MenuSceneWrapper`:

```
@Override
public void populate() {

    MenuScene menuScene = new MenuScene(camera);
    menuScene.getBackground().setColor(0.82f, 0.96f, 0.97f);

        playMenuItem = new ColorMenuItemDecorator(new TextMenuItem(0,
res.font, "PLAY", vbom),
            Color.CYAN, Color.WHITE);

        soundMenuItem = new MyTextMenuItemDecorator(new TextMenuItem(1,
res.font, getSoundLabel(), vbom),
            Color.CYAN, Color.WHITE);

        menuScene.addMenuItem(playMenuItem);
        menuScene.addMenuItem(soundMenuItem);

        menuScene.buildAnimations();
        menuScene.setBackgroundEnabled(true);

        menuScene.setOnMenuItemClickListener(this);

    Sprite player = new Sprite(240, 280, res.playerTextureRegion,
vbom);
    menuScene.attachChild(player);

    Text hiscoreText = new Text(240, 1000, res.font, "HISCORE: " +
activity.getHiScore(), vbom);
    menuScene.attachChild(hiscoreText);

    hiscoreText.registerEntityModifier(
        new SequenceEntityModifier(
            new ParallelEntityModifier(
```

```
                  new MoveYModifier(2f, 1000, 600),
                  new RotationByModifier(2f, 20f)
                  ),
           new RotationByModifier(0.2f, -20f)
           )
      );


      setChildScene(menuScene);


   }
```

First, we changed the position of the high score text to be located beyond the upper border of the screen. Then, we used a sequence. The first part makes the text fall and rotate slightly by 20 degrees clockwise. The second part makes it rotate back to the original position, as shown in the following screenshot:

Modifiers

There are plenty of modifiers to use. Here's a list of the class names of the available modifiers. They have self-explanatory names. Each modifier expects several parameters. There is always the duration parameter, with the exception of chaining modifiers. Then, there are one to three parameters that depend on the type of the modifier. Optionally, we can specify the ease function and the callback hook, which we will see later.

- `MoveModifier`: This simply moves an entity from point A to point B; both points must be specified. Entity will jump to point A if it's at a different location. `MoveXModifier` and `MoveYModifier` are single axis variants of this modifier.

- `MoveByModifier`: This moves an entity from its current position to a new position using the specified x and y values.

- `ScaleModifier`: This changes the size of the entity.

- `RotationModifier`: This rotates the entity from angle A to angle B. There is also `RotationByModifier`.

- `AlphaModifier` and `ColorModifier`: This changes the color or alpha channel of an object.

- `PathModifier`: This is a modifier that is a little bit more complex. It moves an entity along a specified path.

- `DelayModifier`: This does nothing; it simply waits for the specified time. However, it still has the start and finish hooks. This is useful in a sequence.

There are also three curve modifiers that allow us to move an entity along a smooth curve, but the definition of such curves requires some complex math and it is not in the scope of this book.

Ease functions

The effect we have created doesn't look bad. However, what if we wanted the text to bounce a little when it reaches the destination? The answer is to use the easing equations. Now, the text moves along the y axis, 400 pixels downwards, linearly. This is how we make it bounce:

```
hiscoreText.registerEntityModifier(
    new SequenceEntityModifier(
        new ParallelEntityModifier(
            new MoveYModifier(2f, 1000, 600,
```

```
            EaseBounceOut.getInstance()
            ),
        new RotationByModifier(2f, 20f)
        ),
    new RotationByModifier(0.2f, -20f)
    )
);
```

We have added just the easing, nothing else, but suddenly, the effect looks much better. This is because in real life, objects usually don't move at a constant speed; the speed varies as they accelerate or come to rest and sometimes they bounce before coming to rest.

For each easing equation, there are three variants: in, out, and in-out. They mean that the effect is coming at the beginning, end, or both. Here's a graph that compares the linear ease function with the bounce-out, which we have used:

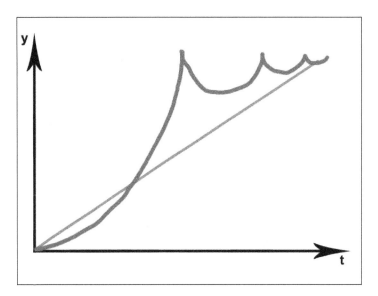

The horizontal axis shows time. The entity starts moving slowly, accelerates, and bounces a few times until it stops.

 To see all available functions, see the hierarchy of the IEntityModifier interface. All graphs can be seen, for example, at http://easings.net/.

Using the modifier callback hooks

Each modifier has one more parameter, a listener that listens to two events, the modifier start and the modifier end. Creating such a listener is very simple. Here is the code that belongs to the populate() method of the MenuSceneWrapper class, just before the line where we create the modifiers:

```
IEntityModifierListener myListener = new IEntityModifierListener()
{

    @Override
    public void onModifierStarted(IModifier<IEntity> pModifier,
IEntity pItem) {
        pItem.setColor(Color.RED);
    }

    @Override
    public void onModifierFinished(IModifier<IEntity> pModifier,
IEntity pItem) {
        pItem.setColor(Color.GREEN);
    }
};
```

The listener is created as an anonymous class that implements the IEntityModifierListener interface. The interface defines two methods: onModifierStarted() and onModifierFinished(). The names are self-explanatory. The parameters available in the methods are the modifier itself (because at the time we are creating the listener, we don't know which modifier it is), and the item that is being a modifier, in our case a text, but it can be a sprite or any other entity.

And here's how to use the listener. Only a small change to the existing code is required:

```
hiscoreText.registerEntityModifier(
    new SequenceEntityModifier(
        new ParallelEntityModifier(
            new MoveYModifier(2f, 1000, 600,
                EaseBounceOut.getInstance()
                ),
            new RotationByModifier(2f, 20f, myListener)
            ),
        new RotationByModifier(0.2f, -20f)
        )
    );
```

We are simply changing the color of the text. At the beginning, we set it to red and when the text has finished falling, we change it to green.

Particle systems

A particle system is a method used to create effects such as fire, smoke, or snow. The technique involves rendering a lot of small particles at once. A particle is a small picture. It's hard to define what it should represent. In the case of snow, it should be a single snowflake. When creating smoke or fire a small fire ball or a puff of smoke would be a good start.

A particle system usually creates a particle at a given point using initial parameters such as scale, opacity, and rotation. A set of modifiers is also created and each particle is modified by all modifiers over time. A particle system also defines the lifespan of a particle and how many particles are to be spawned.

Making particle systems look good is an art and there is no single way to do it. We are going to see how we can create two completely different effects using the same picture. Our game doesn't really need particle systems and so we will add one of these effects to the menu scene just for illustration and we will create a special app to show the other effect. Let's start with the less obvious one.

Creating a flying in the clouds effect

We can create a simple illusion of flying upwards through clouds using a particle system that will spawn clouds on top of the screen and move them downwards.

In AndEngine, the particle system spawning area can be a point, circle, or a rectangle, and either an outline or the whole shape. We will use a rectangle. Let's add the following code to the populate() method of the MenuScreenWrapper class:

```
@Override
public void populate() {

    MenuScene menuScene = new MenuScene(camera);
    menuScene.getBackground().setColor(0.82f, 0.96f, 0.97f);

    float timeToLive = 12f;
    final BatchedSpriteParticleSystem particleSystem = new
BatchedSpriteParticleSystem(
        new RectangleParticleEmitter(192, 900, 300, 0),
        1, 5, 200,
        res.cloud1TextureRegion, vbom);

}
```

We have a lot of constants here. First, we are defining the lifespan of each particle as 12 seconds. Next, we are creating a batched-sprite particle system. Batched sprites are basically the same as separate sprites, but they are all created using a single object and share a lot of properties. For example, all sprites that use the same texture could be batched together. And that's exactly what our sprites in particle systems are—sprites using the same texture.

The performance optimization is happening on a lower level and we don't have to worry about it. Basically, having a batch of sprites that share some properties in a single object instead of a lot of separate sprites means less memory readings, OpenGL calls, and so on.

A batched sprite particle system also uses a special sprite class called `UncoloredSprite`. We will see this in the next code snippet. It doesn't mean that our sprite will be black and white, but it means it has less properties saved in the vertex buffer.

The particle system needs an emitter and we are using a rectangle. It is defined by its centerX and centerY (the center coordinates) and width and height. The center is moved slightly left, because our particle engine spawns the particles using the bottom left corner instead of the center. This is a small bug in AndEngine and so we are using this workaround. We are spawning the particles offscreen to create the desired effect.

The numbers `1`, `5`, and `200` define the spawn rate. The first number is the minimum particles spawned per second and the second number is maximum per second. The third number is maximum particles on screen at a given moment. In our case, it means spawn one to five clouds per second until you reach 200. Unless we remove the particles, no particles will be spawned after 200.

The last parameters state that we are using our cloud texture and the Vertex Buffer Object manager.

Let's continue coding and add the following lines:

```
particleSystem.addParticleInitializer(new VelocityParticleInitializer<
UncoloredSprite>(0, 0, -50, -90));
particleSystem.addParticleInitializer(new ExpireParticleInitializer<Un
coloredSprite>(timeToLive));
```

These are two typical particle initializers. The velocity initializer defines the initial speed range for each particle, in our case, no horizontal movement and something between 50 and 90 pixels per second downwards. The second initializer simply says that each particle should be removed after the specified period, in our case, 12 seconds.

We can add more initializers, for example, one for color, as follows:

```
particleSystem.addParticleInitializer(new ColorParticleInitializer<Unc
oloredSprite>(Color.WHITE, new Color(0.9f, 0.9f, 0.9f)));
```

This will spawn white and slightly colored clouds ranging from the original white cloud to tinted red, green, blue, and color combination clouds.

Now, we will look at the modifiers part. We are going to fade out the cloud just before it expires and is removed. We could also set the expiration time to a longer value and let the clouds expire without the fade out, but let's do the former to see how is it done:

```
particleSystem.addParticleModifier(new AlphaParticleModifier<Uncolored
Sprite>(timeToLive - 1, timeToLive, 1f, 0f));
```

 There is actually a modifier called OffCameraExpireParticleModifier that will dispose of our particles when they reach the bottom of the screen. However, we are already spawning them offscreen, so it wouldn't work. They would be removed immediately after spawning.

Here's how the effect looks:

There's one more setting available for particle systems and that is color blending using the method `particleSystem.setBlendFunction(source, destination)`. When two particles overlap, the final color is calculated and the result is influenced by the blend function. However, in the version of AndEngine we are using, it has no effect in combination with the batched particle system because it uses `UncoloredSprite`.

The blending options for source and destination parameters with examples can be found at `http://www.zeuscmd.com/tutorials/opengles/19-Blending.php`.

The code for this chapter contains a standalone example that uses blending settings to create a fire effect. Let's use a different type of blending to create a really cool effect.

Creating a fire and smoke effect

Two of the most typical effects created using particle systems are fire and smoke. We are going to use a special smoke texture, which looks like this:

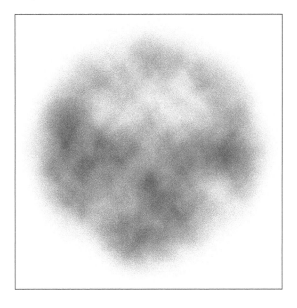

And for fire, we will actually use the same texture, just with a bit of color. We don't need to create another texture. We can use the same smoke texture and use color initialize to turn it red. This is what we need:

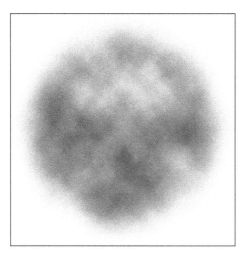

For this example, we will create a new application with a simple black background. Here's the basic skeleton:

```
public class GameActivity extends SimpleBaseGameActivity {

    public static final int CAMERA_WIDTH = 480;
    public static final int CAMERA_HEIGHT = 800;
    public static final int FPS_LIMIT = 30;

    ITexture smokeTex;
    ITextureRegion smokeTexReg;

    @Override
    public Engine onCreateEngine(EngineOptions pEngineOptions) {
        Engine engine = new LimitedFPSEngine(pEngineOptions, FPS_LIMIT);
        engine.registerUpdateHandler(new FPSLogger());
        return engine;
    }

    @Override
    public EngineOptions onCreateEngineOptions() {
        EngineOptions engineOptions;
        Camera camera = new Camera(0, 0, CAMERA_WIDTH, CAMERA_HEIGHT);
        IResolutionPolicy resolutionPolicy = new FillResolutionPolicy();
        engineOptions = new EngineOptions(true, ScreenOrientation.
    PORTRAIT_FIXED, resolutionPolicy, camera);
```

```
engineOptions.setWakeLockOptions(WakeLockOptions.SCREEN_ON);
engineOptions.getRenderOptions().setDithering(true);
return engineOptions;
}

@Override
protected void onCreateResources() throws IOException {
    smokeTex = new AssetBitmapTexture(this.getTextureManager(),
this.getAssets(), "gfx/smoke.png", TextureOptions.BILINEAR_
PREMULTIPLYALPHA);
    smokeTexReg = TextureRegionFactory.extractFromTexture(smokeTex);
    smokeTex.load();
}
@Override
protected Scene onCreateScene() {
    Scene scene = new Scene();
    scene.getBackground().setColor(Color.BLACK);
    createSmoke(scene);
    createFire(scene);
    return scene;
}


}
```

The skeleton app is the same as in our game. We are using the
`SimpleBaseGameActivity` class; so, we don't need to call the callbacks ourselves .
We are also using `LimitedFPSEngine` with the limit set to 30 frames per second.
As particle systems can be very CPU intensive, it's a good idea to limit the number
of frames required to save the battery. We are also loading a single texture resource
and creating a texture region directly from it without any texture atlas.

And now for the two most important methods; we will start with the smoke:

```
private void createSmoke(Scene scene) {
    final BatchedSpriteParticleSystem smokeParticleSystem = new
BatchedSpriteParticleSystem(
        new CircleParticleEmitter(240, 400, 50),
        20, 40, 300,
        smokeTexReg, getVertexBufferObjectManager());

    float ttl = 5.5f;

    smokeParticleSystem.addParticleInitializer(new VelocityParticleIni
tializer<UncoloredSprite>(-25, 25, 20, 60));
```

```
    smokeParticleSystem.addParticleInitializer(new AccelerationParticl
eInitializer<UncoloredSprite>(0, 20));
    smokeParticleSystem.addParticleInitializer(new ExpireParticleIniti
alizer<UncoloredSprite>(ttl));
    smokeParticleSystem.addParticleInitializer(new ScaleParticleInitia
lizer<UncoloredSprite>(0.1f, 0.5f));
    smokeParticleSystem.addParticleInitializer(new RotationParticleIni
tializer<UncoloredSprite>(0f, 360f));

    smokeParticleSystem.addParticleModifier(new OffCameraExpireParticl
eModifier<UncoloredSprite>(getEngine().getCamera()));
    smokeParticleSystem.addParticleModifier(new AlphaParticleModifier<
UncoloredSprite>(0f, 0.5f, 0f, 0.2f));
    smokeParticleSystem.addParticleModifier(new AlphaParticleModifier<
UncoloredSprite>(2f, ttl, 0.2f, 0f));
    scene.attachChild(smokeParticleSystem);
}
```

We are using the `BatchedSpriteParticleSystem` to save performance. In this case, we don't need any special blending options. We are not changing the blending options because the default blending works well for the smoke effect. The default is GL_ONE for source and GL_ZERO for destination. Destination is a color already in the buffer. So it's the first particle drawn there. Then the source is the color being added, the second particle. When the source is GL_ONE and the destination GL_ZERO, it simply means that the destination, the particle drawn first, will be ignored and only the new color, the second particle, will be shown.

This is how the blending looks using three overlaying triangles added in the numbered order:

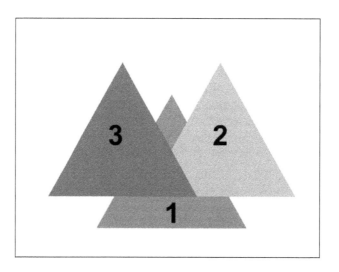

We are spawning the particles in the middle of the screen where we expect the fire to reach. We want the smoke to appear just above the fire. Scale and rotation initializers add randomness to the particles. The velocity initializer makes them shoot upwards and the acceleration initializer makes them speed up to make an illusion of a real smoke.

The modifiers are used to remove smoke particles when they exit the screen and fade them in as they appear and fade out as they reach the top.

The fire effect uses blending and, therefore, we can't use the batched particle system that uses `UncoloredSprite`. We are going to build a less optimized particle system then, using the following code:

```
private void createFire(Scene scene) {
    IEntityFactory<Sprite> ief = new IEntityFactory<Sprite>() {

        @Override
        public Sprite create(float pX, float pY) {
            return new Sprite(pX, pY, smokeTexReg,
getVertexBufferObjectManager());
        }
    };

    final ParticleSystem<Sprite> fireParticleSystem = new
ParticleSystem<Sprite>(ief,
        new PointParticleEmitter(240, 100),
        20, 30, 200);
    fireParticleSystem.addParticleInitializer(new BlendFunctionParticl
eInitializer<Sprite>(GLES20.GL_SRC_ALPHA, GLES20.GL_ONE));
    fireParticleSystem.addParticleInitializer(new ColorParticleInitial
izer<Sprite>(1f, 0.4f, 0.1f));
    fireParticleSystem.addParticleInitializer(new AlphaParticleInitial
izer<Sprite>(0f));

    fireParticleSystem.addParticleInitializer(new VelocityParticleInit
ializer<Sprite>(-15, 15, 20, 90));
    fireParticleSystem.addParticleInitializer(new ExpireParticleInitia
lizer<Sprite>(4.5f));
    fireParticleSystem.addParticleInitializer(new ScaleParticleInitial
izer<Sprite>(0.5f));
    fireParticleSystem.addParticleInitializer(new RotationParticleInit
ializer<Sprite>(0f, 360f));

    fireParticleSystem.addParticleModifier(new AlphaParticleModifier<S
prite>(0f, 0.5f, 0f, 0.2f));
```

```
        fireParticleSystem.addParticleModifier(new AlphaParticleModifier<S
    prite>(3f, 4.5f, 0.2f, 0f));
        fireParticleSystem.addParticleModifier(new ScaleParticleModifier<S
    prite>(3f, 4.5f, 0.5f, 0f));
        scene.attachChild(fireParticleSystem);
    }
```

This particle system requires us to create an entity factory, which is the first line. It's nothing more than a class with one method that returns the representation of the particles, in our case, a simple `Sprite`. The particles are spawned from a single point here and most of the initializers and modifiers should be clear after we build the clouds and smoke systems. The only new thing is `BlendFunctionParticleInitializer`.

We are using `GLES20.GL_SRC_ALPHA`, `GLES20.GL_ONE` blending, which means that the color of the particle already drawn is used and the new particle's color is added to it using its alpha channel.

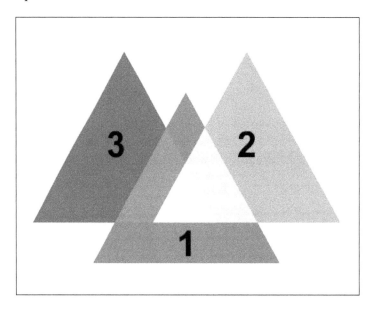

We need this kind of blending to make the center of the fire white. When a lot of particles are drawn on top of each other, their colors add up. We are coloring the smoke particle red with a bit of yellow. That means that when there will be only one particle, the final color will be reddish. When there will be a lot of particles, the final color will be bright orange and yellow, exactly like a real flame. Here's how the final effect looks:

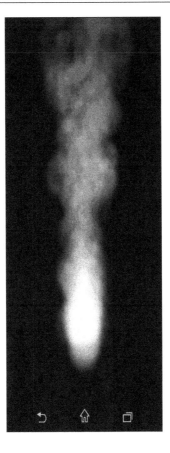

Here's a simple trick that shows you how to make the flame blue. Let's change the color initializer to this:

```
fireParticleSystem.addParticleInitializer(new ColorParticleInitializer
<Sprite>(0.3f, 0.4f, 1f));
```

This will result in coloring the smoke particle medium blue and thanks to the blending options, we will get a blue flame.

There's a lot of blending options available. Not all combinations are viable. It would be impossible to illustrate all combinations on paper, but there are many excellent resources available online. Visit http://www.andersriggelsen.dk/glblendfunc. php for a nice interactive testing tool that offers all the blending options.

When using particle systems, we must be careful not to use too many particles. The smoke and fire effects can spawn thousands of sprites. It can hamper the performance significantly.

Parallax background

When travelling by train, mountains in the distance seem to be static, but trees and grass next to the track move very fast. In 2D games, a similar effect is simulated by a parallax background. It adds a feeling of depth to the game. A parallax background contains a few layers. The player is usually in the front, but there can be a layer in front of the player as well. This simulates objects that are closer to the camera.

When the camera moves, the layers in the back are scrolled slowly and the layers in front are scrolled faster; the same as in our train example.

In platformers, we often use a static background with a few parallax layers. It's a good idea to make the background less prominent and less distracting, but nevertheless beautiful. Some of the layers can move automatically; for example, clouds can move even though the camera is static.

Here's a typical example of a parallax background: a blue sky and a sun as a background, clouds that can move a little, slow scrolling mountains, and fast scrolling grass. The background layers are typically seamlessly wrapped around.

AndEngine offers a horizontal parallax background. It can have an arbitrary number of layers that can move in different speeds. However, we need a vertical parallax background for our game. We will have to create our own class. However, the use of our class is exactly the same as the original parallax background.

VerticalParallaxEntity

In the following example, we will explain how the parallax background with the entities works. To begin, we are going to extend a ParallaxEntity class:

```
public class VerticalParallaxEntity extends ParallaxEntity {

  IEntity entity;
  float parallaxFactor;

  public VerticalParallaxEntity(float parallaxFactor, IEntity entity)
{
    super(parallaxFactor, entity);
    this.entity = entity;
    this.parallaxFactor = parallaxFactor;
  }

  public void onDraw(final GLState pGLState, final Camera pCamera,
final float pParallaxValue) {
    pGLState.pushModelViewGLMatrix();
    {
      final float cameraHeight = pCamera.getHeight();
      final float entityHeightScaled = entity.getHeight() * entity.
getScaleY();
      float baseOffset = (pParallaxValue * parallaxFactor) %
entityHeightScaled;

      while (baseOffset > 0) {
        baseOffset -= entityHeightScaled;
      }
      pGLState.translateModelViewGLMatrixf(0, baseOffset, 0);

      float currentMaxY = baseOffset;

      do {
        entity.onDraw(pGLState, pCamera);
        pGLState.translateModelViewGLMatrixf(0, entityHeightScaled,
0);
        currentMaxY += entityHeightScaled;
      } while (currentMaxY < cameraHeight);
    }
    pGLState.popModelViewGLMatrix();
  }
}
```

The code for the layer might seem a bit intimidating. It deals with low-level OpenGL calls. The highlighted code is the most important part. The `onDraw()` method first measures the camera height and the real height of the entity. Then there are two float numbers: parallax value and parallax factor. The value says how much the camera moved. It can be an arbitrary number and we will be passing the camera's *y* coordinate. The factor determines how much should the entity (layer) move.

We are setting the factor at the beginning when we create this entity. In our case, a positive number means scrolling the layer in the same direction as the camera and negative number scrolls it in the opposite way. Zero would mean a static layer. The higher the absolute number, the faster the scroll speed. So, in our case, we need numbers between 0 and -1.

Creating a parallax background

The code that creates the background belongs to the `GameScene` class. It replaces our old static background. First, let's add a method to create it:

```
private void createParallaxBackground() {
    parallaxBackground = new ParallaxBackground(0.82f, 0.96f, 0.97f);

    // layer in the back
    Entity clouds = new Entity();
    clouds.setSize(480, 800);
    clouds.setAnchorCenter(0, 0);
    Sprite cloud1 = new Sprite(200, 300, res.cloud1TextureRegion,
vbom);
    Sprite cloud2 = new Sprite(300, 600, res.cloud2TextureRegion,
vbom);
    clouds.attachChild(cloud1);
    clouds.attachChild(cloud2);

    VerticalParallaxEntity cloudsLayer = new VerticalParallaxEntity(-
0.1f, clouds);
    parallaxBackground.attachParallaxEntity(cloudsLayer);

    //layer in front
    Entity platforms = new Entity();
    platforms.setSize(480, 800);
    platforms.setAnchorCenter(0, 0);
    Sprite platform1 = new Sprite(150, 200, res.platformTextureRegion,
vbom);
    platform1.setColor(0.3f, 0.3f, 0.3f, 0.3f);
    platform1.setScale(0.8f);
```

```
    Sprite platform2 = new Sprite(250, 550, res.platformTextureRegion,
vbom);
    platform2.setColor(0.3f, 0.3f, 0.3f, 0.3f);
    platform2.setScale(0.8f);
    Sprite platform3 = new Sprite(350, 450, res.platformTextureRegion,
vbom);
    platform3.setColor(0.3f, 0.3f, 0.3f, 0.3f);
    platform3.setScale(0.8f);
    platforms.attachChild(platform1);
    platforms.attachChild(platform2);
    platforms.attachChild(platform3);

    VerticalParallaxEntity platformsLayer = new
VerticalParallaxEntity(-0.5f, platforms);
    parallaxBackground.attachParallaxEntity(platformsLayer);

    setBackground(parallaxBackground);
}
```

Our background has two layers. Each layer can be a single image (a sprite) or an entity assembled from multiple objects. We are doing the latter. The first layer is a very slow moving layer with two clouds. We also set the size of the entity and its center, because the parallax background needs to know the size to correctly wrap around the layer. The second layer is assembled from three semi-transparent and scaled-down platforms. They will appear as if they are in the background and we will make them move a bit slower than the camera.

We must also change the populate() method to use this background:

```
    private ParallaxBackground parallaxBackground;

    @Override
    public void populate() {
//      createBackground();
        createParallaxBackground();
        createPlayer();
    ...
    }
```

And finally, we must be passing the parallax value to the background in each update cycle to make it scroll properly:

```
    @Override
    protected void onManagedUpdate(float pSecondsElapsed) {
        super.onManagedUpdate(pSecondsElapsed);
```

```
parallaxBackground.setParallaxValue(camera.getCenterY());

boolean added = false;
...
}
```

The final effect is that the clouds move very slowly and the platforms in the back move a bit faster but still slower than the platforms that the player can use. In the following screenshot, we can see how the platforms are wrapped (the top background platform is visible both on top and the bottom):

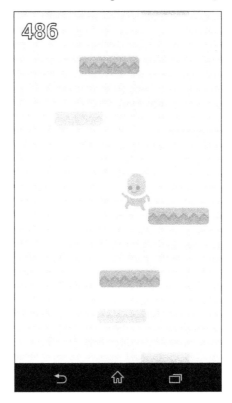

Shaders

Shaders are little programs that can be run on the prepared geometry (vertices) or rendered **fragments** just before they get rendered on screen. Fragments are like pixels before they get thrown on the screen.

Shaders can create amazing effects by displacing vertices, coloring fragments, and so on. It's the most advanced topic that appears in this book, but every game developer should know that they exist.

Every entity, in fact, already uses a very simple vertex and fragment shader program that doesn't do anything than to display the correct geometry with the correct color. The shapes use a single color and the sprites use texture coordinates.

We are going to create a very simple shader program that will turn our platforms black and white.

The code for the shader programs is long and it contains low level OpenGL calls. We will use the basic shader program available in AndEngine and modify it a little. The new program class is called `BWShaderProgram`. It contains a simple vertex shader that does exactly the same thing as the basic one. The only change is the fragment shader.

Shaders in OpenGL are written in a domain-specific language called GLSL. We are storing the program as a simple string. Here's the relevant part:

```
public static final String FRAGMENTSHADER =
    "precision lowp float;\n" +
    "uniform sampler2D " + ShaderProgramConstants.UNIFORM_TEXTURE_0
+ ";\n" +
    "varying mediump vec2 " + ShaderProgramConstants.VARYING_
TEXTURECOORDINATES + ";\n" +
    "void main() {\n" +
    "  vec4 myColor = texture2D(" + ShaderProgramConstants.UNIFORM_
TEXTURE_0 + ", " + ShaderProgramConstants.VARYING_TEXTURECOORDINATES +
");\n" +
    "  gl_FragColor.r = dot(myColor.rgb, vec3(.3, .59, .11));\n" +
    "  gl_FragColor.g = dot(myColor.rgb, vec3(.3, .59, .11));\n" +
    "  gl_FragColor.b = dot(myColor.rgb, vec3(.3, .59, .11));\n" +
    "  gl_FragColor.a = myColor.a;\n" +
    "}";
```

The program first defines a few variables that we are going to need. Then it looks up the correct texture pixel (**texel**) in the texture and calculates red, green, and blue values to be the same. This will make the final fragment, and therefore, the pixel monochromatic as well.

The shader program must be loaded during the resource loading phase and loaded only once. We will add it to the `ResouceManager` class in the `loadGameGraphics()` method, as follows:

```
public BWShaderProgram myShaderProgram;
public void loadGameGraphics() {
    ...

    myShaderProgram = BWShaderProgram.getInstance();
```

```
        activity.getShaderProgramManager().loadShaderProgram(myShaderProg
    ram);
    }
```

To use this shader program instead of the default one, let's change the
`PlatformFactory` class:

```
    public Platform createPlatform(float x, float y) {
        Platform platform = new Platform(x, y, ResourceManager.
    getInstance().platformTextureRegion, vbom);
        platform.setShaderProgram(ResourceManager.getInstance().
    myShaderProgram);

        ...
    }
```

And that's it! Now our platforms are displayed using our custom shader program.
Here's how it looks (the background platforms are not affected because they
are not created using the factory):

The AndEngine examples project that comes with AndEngine demonstrates a radial blur shader.

Summary

This was the final chapter before we will release our game. We learned what polishing is and how we can polish our game with respect to audiovisuals. Music was added to our game in this chapter and some special effects were demonstrated. We learned how to improve simple tweens by using easing functions. We saw what a particle system can do. Our background was changed to a parallax background and we implemented our own vertical parallax background as an addition to the AndEngine horizontal scrolling parallax background. Finally, we introduced shaders and saw a simple example of what they can do.

In the next chapter, we will wrap up our game and publish it. We will discuss what happens after the game is published and what is needed to make a game successful.

11
Testing, Publishing, and What's Next

After the game is completed and tested on a developer's device, it's still far from finished. A successful game must be thoroughly tested on a wide selection of devices, and it also has to be marketed. After the game is published, it also needs to be supported and newly-found bugs must be fixed promptly.

In this final chapter, we will learn how to test the game on different devices with minimal resources and how to set up user testing with the help of the community. We are also going to see how to publish a game and discuss some basic ways of promoting the game. Lastly, we are going to learn how to deal with a user's feedback after the game is published.

Creating a production APK

The first thing that must be done is creating a production APK. The difference between a developer and production version is that the developer one is signed by a debug certificate while the production one is signed by its own certificate. This is necessary to identify an APK in the store with something that is hard to duplicate.

The certificate can be a **self-signed** certificate, which means we are going to create it ourselves and we don't need to use a certificate from a certification authority.

The following are the steps needed to create a production certificate and sign it with a newly-created certificate:

1. We are going to use the **Export** option in the project context menu available after right-clicking on the project name in the **Project Explorer** window in Eclipse. First, we select the right export option, which is hidden under **Android | Export Android Application**. This is shown in the following screenshot:

2. After clicking on the **Next** button, the wizard checks our game for errors. There should be no errors at this time, as shown in the following screenshot:

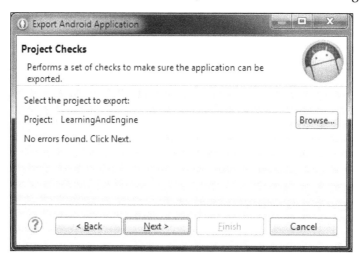

3. After clicking on the **Next** button, we are going to create our own new **keystore**, which is a file storage that holds all of our encrypted keys. After selecting a location and typing a new password, we can continue in the export wizard. This is shown in the following screenshot. We only need one keystore for all games. It's important to use a strong password and to never lose your keystore. Saving it in cloud storage might be a good idea. If the keystore is lost, your game can never be updated again.

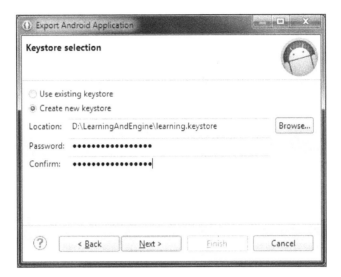

4. In the next step, a certificate for our game is created in our keystore. A few fields must be filled in, as shown in the following screenshot. The **Alias** field will have the name of the certificate used to identify it in the keystore. Each certificate will need a password. The **Validity (years)** field must have a value that exceeds the expected lifespan of the game, and right now, the requirement is that the certificate is valid until the year 2033. At least one field that identifies the author must be filled in. For each game, create a separate certificate.

5. The last page of the wizard only wants us to select a location of the new APK, as shown in the following screenshot:

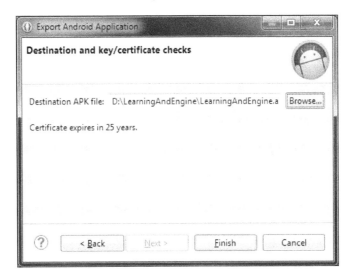

The whole process takes some time and it is CPU intensive. At the end, a new keystore is created with the new certificate and the production APK is created as well, signed by it.

Often when updating the APK, the export ends with an error stating **Conversion to Dalvik format failed with error 1**. There is no simple cure for this error. Cleaning and building the project from scratch and removing temporary files from the system and the bin and gen directories from the project usually help. To prevent certain issues, turning off the auto build is an option as well.

Testing with the production APK

It's always a good idea to uninstall the debug version of the game from the device and install the production version. We should never publish the APK without checking it first even if the changes made were simple, because the export process, in rare cases, introduces errors to the APK.

To install the APK, the adb command-line tool is used. The **Unknown sources** option must be enabled in the security settings of the device. The APK can be installed using the following command:

```
adb install LearningAndEngine.apk
```

 You can also send the APK to yourself via e-mail. Opening the attachment in a Gmail app will let you install the APK.

Testing on multiple devices

It is necessary to test the game on as many different devices as possible. The game might look and feel very different on tablets and phones and even on two similar phones. Moreover, some phones define their own ways of handling the application life cycle, especially pausing and resuming. Testing on a few major brands and popular devices is always recommended.

Using an emulator

Testing on different devices is not always an option for many reasons. In that case, we should test at least a few different resolutions in an emulator. An emulator can never substitute testing on a real device. It is missing many features of phones and tablets and, of course, even the implemented functionality is just an emulation.

To run the game on an emulator, first start the **Android Virtual Device Manager** from Eclipse. The option is located in the main button bar and in the **Window** menu.

In the current version of the SDK, we have two options: creating a new device or cloning an emulation of an existing device. We will create a new one. Let's click on the **New** button in the manager and create a new phone emulation. We will be presented with the window shown in the following screenshot:

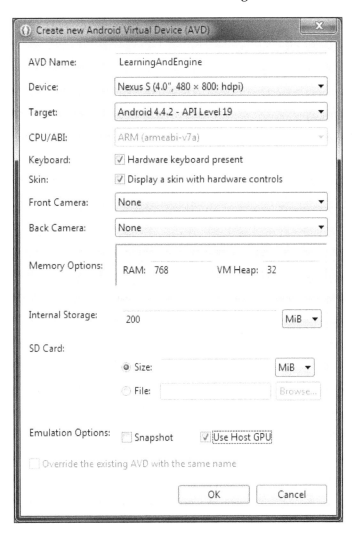

The parameters used are just an example, but the device will do just fine. The resolution will fit nicely on the screen. We are using the latest available Android SDK, at the time of writing this book. The **RAM** parameter should be set to at least 512 MB in order to run the latest Android somewhat smoothly. The **Use Host GPU** option means that the graphics will be emulated on a graphics card instead of the CPU, which usually brings a significant performance boost. However, the built-in emulator is still quite slow even on the latest machines.

> As an alternative, we can use the Genymotion emulator or install the HAXM Intel driver and Intel Atom Android images. Genymotion is a virtual machine, which performs better than the built-in emulator, and the HAXM driver uses hardware virtualization to speed up the bundled emulator to run faster.

After creating the device, it appears in the run dialog and we can run our game the same way as we did on the real device, as shown in the following screenshot. We can use the adb command-line tool and install the production APK in the emulator as well.

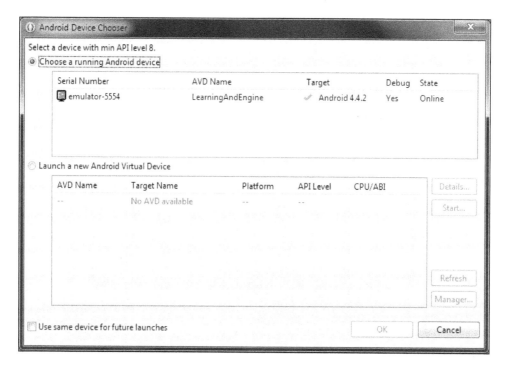

The following screenshot shows how it looks when our game runs successfully in the emulator:

Getting in touch with the community

During the making of a game, we often get stuck. Fortunately, AndEngine has an active community that can help us resolve our problems. From a long-term view, it's also beneficial to give back to the community. One of the easiest ways is to give feedback on other developers' games. Creating a circle of friends in the community is always beneficial later on when you need to test your game with other people.

The community forums are located at `http://www.andengine.org/forums/`. There are also many sites with AndEngine tutorials. The best known is Mathew's tutorial website, which can be found at `http://www.matim-dev.com/`. You can also visit my website for more tutorials at `http://android.kul.is/`.

We can find more help in other game development communities that aren't directly associated with AndEngine. For example, `http://www.stackoverflow.com` is a good website for asking questions about programming.

Publishing the game to the Google Play store

There are many Android stores available and distributing your game yourself is an option too, but the biggest and most popular store is still the Google Play store and therefore, every developer should use it.

The official documentation for developers contains a handy *Get started* guide and is available at `https://support.google.com/googleplay/android-developer/`.

Publishing to the beta stage first

Setting up a Google Play store alpha and beta test is not directly related to AndEngine, but every Android developer should know about this great option to test games and apps directly in the store.

Moreover, the publishing process in the alpha and beta stage is the same as in the production stage, making it easy to try the whole life cycle first. The alpha and beta versions are basically the same. However, the store allows us to maintain three different versions and make them available to different people at the same time. The alpha and beta stages allow us to define a group of people who can download the APK. The production version is different, because an APK published as production will be publicly available.

The alpha and beta stages are available to members of a selected Google Group or Google+ community. Therefore, creating a small Google+ community and adding trusted users to it is one of the best ways to test the game on different devices.

We won't describe the process here in detail because the official documentation offers a detailed manual to perform each step. However, here's a quick summary.

Creating the application

First, we need to create a new application. This is done on the **ALL APPLICATIONS** page, as shown in the following screenshot:

The console will ask for a name and whether we want to start with uploading the APK or preparing the store listing, as shown in the following screenshot. We need to perform both steps before publication; therefore, choosing which step to perform first depends on your personal preferences.

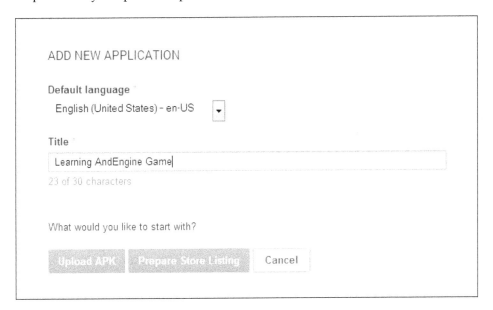

Let's start with the store listing. We must fill in the fields in the **Pricing & Distribution** and **Store Listing** pages. After that, we can upload our APK. We don't have to worry about the contents now, but it's a good practice to fill everything as if this was the real production version already. That way, we can get feedback on the store listing as well.

The pricing and distribution depends solely on the purpose of our game. For this game, we will set the price to free and make it available in all countries.

For the store listing, we will need at least two screenshots from our game and a high resolution icon. We haven't created an icon yet. However, we can use the following image for now:

We should also replace the launcher icons. So far, we have used the generic Android icon. The source code for this chapter contains the previous image resized to different resolutions in the `res` folder of our game.

 When creating a new application, we can select a single image to serve as our game's icon, and it will be resized automatically. To do it later, we simply replace the generic icon in the `res` folder and its respective resolution's subfolders with our own.

To generate the icons for all resolutions, we can use Android Asset Studio, which is available at `http://romannurik.github.io/AndroidAssetStudio/`.

The Google Play store also requires consent whether the application meets Android content guidelines and an acknowledgement that the application might be subject to US laws. Refer to `https://play.google.com/about/developer-content-policy.html` and `https://support.google.com/googleplay/android-developer/answer/113770` for more information. After this, we can upload our APK to the beta phase.

 Some actions can be performed only after the APK is uploaded. It might be necessary to visit each page multiple times until all pages show a green tick.

When the upload finishes, we should see something like what is shown in the following screenshot:

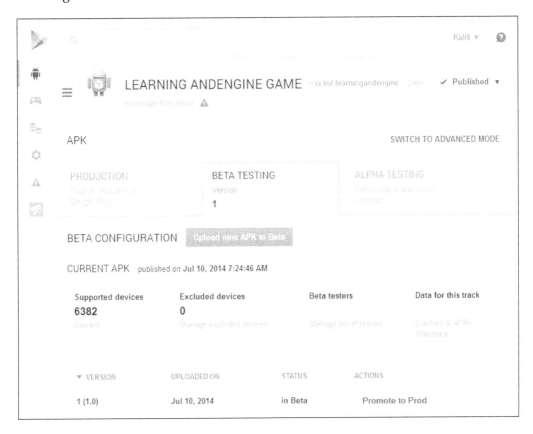

On this page, we can see the version of the APK, which is set to **1**. Every time we upload a new APK, we must increase the version number in the `AndroidManifest.xml` file. This can be done as follows:

```
<manifest xmlns:android="http://schemas.android.
    com/apk/res/android"
    package="is.kul.learningandengine"
    android:versionCode="1"
    android:versionName="1.0" >
```

The `versionCode` value is the right value. It is an integer. The `versionName` value will be displayed in the store listing.

We can also exclude some devices and make our game unavailable for them. This is useful in the case of some nonstandard Android devices or devices with low memory that could theoretically run our game, but in practice, the game will always crash.

Finally, the **Manage list of testers** link allows us to define the users who can access this beta APK. For our game, a public Google+ community was created. It is called *Learning AndEngine* and it can be accessed directly from `https://plus.google.com/communities/105620828467852624663`.

After publishing the game in the beta stage, a special page will be available for testers to access the game at `https://play.google.com/apps/testing/is.kul.learningandengine`.

The APK published in the beta test will be kept available for future reference. It will not be updated. You can find the most recent official version of the game at `https://play.google.com/store/apps/details?id=is.kul.learningandengine.official`.

The **Crashes & ANRs** and **Statistics** links lead to tracking of the said application for the beta stage only.

Crash reports

Crash and **application not responding** (**ANR**) reports show us when our application crashed, on what device, and why. The crash report can also contain a user message, and it typically contains an exception that caused the crash; this is shown in the following screenshot. In the current version of the Google Play store, there are separate reports for each stage.

The alpha and beta testers should fill in the user message describing the action they were performing just before the crash.

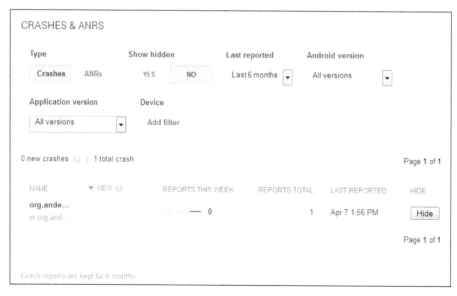

Debugging crashes

Because each crash is typically related to an exception, we can go directly to the code and fix the problem. The application can be run in the debugging mode, where we have an option to stop at a **breakpoint**. A breakpoint is a line of code where we want to stop the execution of the program. After stopping at a breakpoint, we can analyze the current contents of the stack. Learning how to debug Java applications is a useful skill that can help us deal with crashes.

Publishing to production

Publishing to production is basically the same as publishing to the beta or alpha stage. Moreover, we have an option to promote the beta or alpha APK to production APK. There is only one store listing, and we should take special care to make it descriptive and interesting to potential players.

Promotion

Even if we create a great game, it might never be discovered. Marketing a game may take serious effort and should not be underestimated. Most people discover games by searching the Google Play store and, therefore, using the right keywords in the description is very important. However, the Google Play store search option shows games with a lot of downloads higher in the results and because of that, we need to get some initial momentum going and get as many installs as possible. Social networks and game developer communities are probably the best free options and there are of course always paid advertisements.

Marketing is out of scope for this book, but we should pay attention to it. A good marketing strategy begins long before the game is published.

Next steps

It would be a mistake to just sit back and relax after publishing the game to production. If we have done the marketing right, we can see a lot of installs and that means a lot of different people with different phones installing our game. It is almost guaranteed that there will be crashes even after thorough testing.

The first week

In the first few days after the first installs start rolling, we should be ready to fix any errors that might occur quickly and promptly upload the updated version. Bugs in the initial stage can ruin an otherwise good game.

The first month

The game is considered new for exactly thirty days from the publication to production. A new game can appear in lists such as "Top New Free Games" and so on. Appearing in such lists usually means our game will become even more popular. It's therefore important to focus on marketing the game as much as possible in the first month.

 The lists are separate for each country. It might be a good idea to focus on getting into a "Top New" list only in some countries. For example, translating the store description into several languages can help.

Summary

In this chapter, we have discussed some aspects of game development that might not be directly related to AndEngine, but are nevertheless important. Testing on multiple devices and in an emulator, user tests, and publishing are all integral parts of game development and the same can be said for marketing.

Joining a community of game developers might help us not only when we get stuck while making the game, but later as well when we need to test the game and when we need to give our game the first push, to get it out there and get it discovered.

This concludes the whole development life cycle of a game. This chapter's source code is the final source code of the game, which has been published in the Google Play store.

Index

touchscreen
    about 99, 102
    entity touch area 104, 105
    scene touch listener 103, 104
    touch area bindings 106
    touch events 102, 103
tweens 101

U

unsupported languages
    alternatives 84
user input
    about 102
    accelerometer 106-108
    touchscreen 102

V

values, storing
    about 204
    high score 210
    preferences, using 205
    settings 206, 208

VBO 51
vbom (Vertex Buffer Object Manager) 169
vector graphics format 39
velocity
    setting 141, 142
verbose 96
version control system (VCS) 12
Vertex Buffer Object *See* VBO
VerticalParallaxEntity 235

W

warning 96
WebP 42
weld joint 185
what a terrible failure (WTF) 94
wraparound 36, 159
writing systems
    rendering, issues 84

Thank you for buying
Learning AndEngine

About Packt Publishing

Packt, pronounced 'packed', published its first book "*Mastering phpMyAdmin for Effective MySQL Management*" in April 2004 and subsequently continued to specialize in publishing highly focused books on specific technologies and solutions.

Our books and publications share the experiences of your fellow IT professionals in adapting and customizing today's systems, applications, and frameworks. Our solution based books give you the knowledge and power to customize the software and technologies you're using to get the job done. Packt books are more specific and less general than the IT books you have seen in the past. Our unique business model allows us to bring you more focused information, giving you more of what you need to know, and less of what you don't.

Packt is a modern, yet unique publishing company, which focuses on producing quality, cutting-edge books for communities of developers, administrators, and newbies alike. For more information, please visit our website: www.packtpub.com.

About Packt Open Source

In 2010, Packt launched two new brands, Packt Open Source and Packt Enterprise, in order to continue its focus on specialization. This book is part of the Packt Open Source brand, home to books published on software built around Open Source licenses, and offering information to anybody from advanced developers to budding web designers. The Open Source brand also runs Packt's Open Source Royalty Scheme, by which Packt gives a royalty to each Open Source project about whose software a book is sold.

Writing for Packt

We welcome all inquiries from people who are interested in authoring. Book proposals should be sent to author@packtpub.com. If your book idea is still at an early stage and you would like to discuss it first before writing a formal book proposal, contact us; one of our commissioning editors will get in touch with you.

We're not just looking for published authors; if you have strong technical skills but no writing experience, our experienced editors can help you develop a writing career, or simply get some additional reward for your expertise.

Cocos2d-X by Example Beginner's Guide

ISBN: 978-1-78216-734-1   Paperback: 246 pages

Make fun games for any platform using C++, combined with one of the most popular open source frameworks in the world

1. Learn to build multi-device games in simple, easy steps, letting the framework do all the heavy lifting.

2. Spice things up in your games with easy to apply animations, particle effects, and physics simulation.

3. Quickly implement and test your own gameplay ideas, with an eye for optimization and portability.

AndEngine for Android Game Development Cookbook

ISBN: 978-1-84951-898-7   Paperback: 380 pages

Over 70 highly effective recipes with real-world examples to get to grips with the powerful capabilities of AndEngine and GLES 2

1. Step by step detailed instructions and information on a number of AndEngine functions, including illustrations and diagrams for added support and results.

2. Learn all about the various aspects of AndEngine with prime and practical examples, useful for bringing your ideas to life.

3. Improve the performance of past and future game projects with a collection of useful optimization tips.

iOS 7 Game Development

ISBN: 978-1-78355-157-6   Paperback: 120 pages

Develop powerful, engaging games with ready-to-use utilities from Sprite Kit

1. Pen your own endless runner game using Apple's new Sprite Kit framework.

2. Enhance your user experience with easy-to-use animations and particle effects using Xcode 5.

3. Utilize particle systems and create custom particle effects.

iPhone Game Blueprints

ISBN: 978-1-84969-026-3   Paperback: 358 pages

Develop amazing games, visual charts, plots, and graphics for your iPhone

1. Seven step by step game projects for you to build.

2. Cover all aspects from graphics to game ergonomics.

3. Tips and tricks for all of your iPhone programming.

Please check **www.PacktPub.com** for information on our titles